Progress Monitoring Assessments

ELD Unit Tests

Teacher's Manual

Glenview, Illinois • Boston, Massachusetts • Chandler, Arizona • Upper Saddle River, New Jersey

ISBN-13: 978-0-328-63487-3
ISBN-10: 0-328-63487-5
1 2 3 4 5 6 7 8 9 10 V042 14 13 12 11 10

ISBN-13: 978-0-328-63487-3
ISBN-10: 0-328-63487-5

EAN
9 780328 634873
90000 >

CONTENTS

About Progress Monitoring Assessments

The Pearson *Language Central Progress Monitoring Assessments* are designed to monitor child progress and inform teachers of the effectiveness of their instruction. The tests are administered at the end of each of the six units in the program. This Teacher's Manual provides information for administering the Unit Tests, scoring the tests, and interpreting the results.

PURPOSE

The purpose of the *Progress Monitoring Assessment* Unit Tests are to provide feedback to teachers and grade-level teams about the effectiveness of instruction in meeting child learning goals. The assessments are intended to provide a tool for supporting diagnostic efforts, documentation of progress, and potential remediation efforts aimed at improving English language learners' knowledge and abilities. The assessments are scaled to address a range of language ability from *early intermediate* to *early advanced*, with the highest percentage of items (approximately 75%) designed to reflect the *intermediate* level of English language proficiency. These progress-monitoring assessments are based on the content taught in each themed unit and previously taught skills and strategies.

CONNECTION TO PEARSON *READING STREET*

The assessment content is intended to build on the content to which children are exposed in Pearson *Reading Street*. The English learner is exposed to material that is conceptually similar yet streamlined to allow for accurate assessment of discrete skills or deficiencies. As the progress of the English learner class is evaluated and monitored, this information may be used to help predict how these children may perform in the *Reading Street* Program classroom and identify trouble areas needing additional support.

ENGLISH LEARNER PLACEMENT/DIAGNOSTICS

Initial Placement: Several factors must be taken into consideration for the initial placement of the English learner. Often individual skills are not uniformly developed (i.e., a child's listening and speaking skills may be more advanced than his or her reading and writing skills). Typically, when a child functions at different levels in different areas of skill, the lowest functioning level should inform the decision of initial placement. Test scores measure a broad spectrum of linguistic development and thus using a compilation of cut-off scores, rather than a single measure, is recommended. The range of scores can be utilized to assign a starting level.

Benchmark scores from a variety of standardized tests can be used to create a range for initial placement. Currently there are a number of reliable tests available, including:

- Stanford English Language Proficiency Test (Pearson Education)
- TABE Complete Language Assessment System (CTB/McGraw-Hill)
- BEST/BEST Plus (Center for Applied Linguistics)
- LAS/LAS-Links (CTB/McGraw-Hill)
- IPT Title III Testing System (Ballard & Tighe Publishers)
- Woodcock-Muñoz Language Survey (Riverside Publishing Company)
- Bilingual Verbal Ability Tests or BVAT (Riverside Publishing Company)

It may be helpful to factor background information in addition to test scores, such as:

- level of previous education,
- length of time in the United States,
- previous study in other English language programs or other instructional programs, and
- extent of reading and writing skills in the primary language.

Alternative Assessment (classroom testing): Alternative classroom assessment is an informal yet reliable solution to the need for evaluation at the classroom level. Informal assessment may take the form of a performance-focused classroom activity that may include such tools as surveys, learner interviews, checklists, observation tools, learner self-assessments, portfolios, and other classroom-based systems by which a teacher can gather samples of performance.

For example, an assessment may consist of a sorting activity that requires children to perform two distinct tasks: (1) identify and sort photographs in two groups—children determine whether the photographs represent something that contains a specific consonant sound; (2) demonstrate their comprehension of the task and complete the sorting chart—children place the pictures of objects in their respective categories (with the consonant sound or without). Children can be assessed individually based on their completed sorting chart. Acceptable accuracy should be 80% or more of the words by their initial phoneme.

Confirming Placement: After completing the language assessment process, the program options should be carefully considered in order to provide each individual with the least restrictive environment possible. Teachers should verify the initial placement of an English learner once the assessment is complete and the child has started the instructional program. Upon observation, if initial placement seems inappropriate, adjustments may need to be made.

MONITORING THE PROGRESS OF ENGLISH LEARNERS

Children whose native language is not English present unique challenges to educators as they administer and score formal assessments, interpret scores, and make decisions based on test scores. Although many English language learners quickly master social English, the conversational language skills and conventions used in everyday interactions with classmates, they frequently encounter difficulty with the academic English found on formal assessments. The performance of these children is greatly affected by:

- the increasing linguistic demands of vocabulary, including specialized terms, multiple-meaning words, and abstract concepts, and
- structural analysis constraints at the word, sentence, paragraph, and text levels.

Support and Accommodations: There are a number of ways to accommodate the needs of English language learners to ensure fairness and full participation in this program. A general rule of thumb is to use the same accommodations in testing situations as used in instruction. For instance, if children receive part of their instruction in their home language, then it is appropriate to translate test directions and comprehension questions into that language. Acceptable accommodations might include:

- providing additional testing time and allowing frequent or extended breaks,
- administering the tests at times most beneficial to the children,
- administering the tests in small groups or in one-on-one settings,
- reading test directions to children in English or in the child's home languages, and repeating as needed,
- simplifying the language and sentence structure of test directions,

- requesting that children restate and clarify test directions in their own words,
- discussing the pictures and any graphics, such as maps, to ensure that children can interpret them,
- allowing the use of bilingual dictionaries,
- repeatedly reading the test passages orally as often as necessary when listening comprehension is being assessed,
- reading comprehension questions orally to children in English or in their home languages, and
- allowing children to respond orally to questions or dictate answers for transcription.

In providing accommodations to children, it is important not to compromise the intent of the assessment. Keep the following points in mind:

- Do not read the comprehension passages aloud to children except where teachers have the option of assessing listening or reading comprehension. Please refer to the appropriate unit's Teacher's Instructions for specific instructions.
- Do not translate comprehension passages into the child's home language.
- When assessing English vocabulary and grammar skills, do not translate test items into the child's home language.
- When assessing children's writing ability in English, do not transcribe their oral responses to the writing prompts.

These practices would alter the constructs of the assessments. For example, the reading comprehension assessments are designed to measure both word recognition and understanding, so reading the selections to children would actually change the intent of the test.

Following the administration of the formal assessments, it is important to note which accommodations were used for the English learners, and to interpret scores with that information in mind. The National Assessment of Education Progress, a project of the U.S. Department of Education, provides direction on the types of accommodations English learners can receive, specifically when assessed on reading and writing.

Accommodations for English Language Learners		
Direct Linguistic Support		
	Reading	Writing
Has directions read aloud/repeated in English or receives assistance to understand directions	yes	yes
Has directions *only* read aloud in native language	no	no
Has test materials read aloud in native language	no	no
Uses a bilingual version of the booklet (Spanish/English only)	no	no
Uses a bilingual word-for-word dictionary without definitions	no	yes
Has *occasional* words or phrases read aloud in English	no	yes
Has *all* or *most* of the test materials read aloud in English	no	yes
Has oral or written responses in native language translated into written English	no	no
Has directions read aloud/repeated in English or receives assistance to understand directions[1]	yes	yes
Has directions *only* read aloud in native language	no	no
Has test materials read aloud in native language	no	no
Indirect Linguistic Support		
Takes the test in small group (5 or fewer)	yes	yes
Takes the test one-on-one	yes	yes
Receives preferential seating	yes	yes
Has test administered by familiar person	yes	yes
Receives extended time	yes	yes
Is given breaks during the test	yes	yes
Takes test session over several days	no	no

[1] Further information and studies on the validity of the accommodations can be found at the following National Center Education Statistics website (www.nces.ed.gov).

About Passages With Illustrations: The illustrations that accompany comprehension passages are part of the assessment and not considered an accommodation. The illustrations serve two primary purposes. They create a framework for comprehension, and they provide support in following the structure of the written text. Children can use the content of an illustration to develop associations with personal experience, be it social or academic. Children also focus on the illustrations as additional context for the story, particularly when their knowledge of sound-letter/word correspondence in the target language is lacking.

Overview of Pearson *Language Central* Unit Tests – Grade 1

UNIT	R	1	2	3	4	5
Grade 1	Comprehension Checking Skills Word Analysis Vocabulary Writing	Comprehension Checking Skills Word Analysis Vocabulary Writing	Comprehension Checking Skills Word Analysis Vocabulary Writing Fluency	Comprehension Checking Skills Word Analysis Vocabulary Writing Fluency	Comprehension Checking Skills Word Analysis Vocabulary Writing Fluency	Comprehension Checking Skills Word Analysis Vocabulary Writing Fluency

ADMINISTERING THE TESTS

The Progress Monitoring Assessments are designed for group administration. You may decide to administer each test in one sitting, or you may administer parts of the test in two or more sittings. Specific directions for each section of the test are provided in this manual. Directions in bold type are intended to be read aloud to the children. All other directions are intended for your information only.

These tests, except for fluency, are not intended to be timed. We recommend allowing ample time for all children to complete the tests at their own pace. However, for the purposes of scheduling, planning, and practicing timed-test situations, the charts below show the number of items in each test part and the suggested amount of time to be allotted for the completion of each section.

Test Section	Number of Items	Estimated Time
Comprehension	10	30–45 minutes
Checking Skills	10	20 minutes
Word Analysis	10	20–30 minutes
Vocabulary	10	20–30 minutes
Writing	1 prompt	15–20 minutes
Fluency	1 passage	1 minute (timed)

Before Test Day: Review the general test directions in this manual. Modify the test directions as needed according to how you decide to administer each test. Make sufficient copies of the fluency passage so there is one for each child.

On Test Day: Distribute a test to each child. Have children write their names on the front of their test booklets and on any additional papers they may use. Have children follow along as you point out the sections of the test, the titles of the reading passages, and the types of items in each test section: multiple-choice items with 3 answer choices and constructed response items with answer lines. For the sections that require children to write in their test booklets, demonstrate to the children what they must do. When administering the writing sections you may provide any additional paper needed for planning. Explain to the children that only the writing they do on the lined spaces in their test booklets will be scored. Allow time for children to ask questions about the test content and organization before you begin the test.

After Testing: When children have finished the test, collect all test booklets and/or answer sheets. Proceed to score the tests according to the directions provided in each unit section of this manual. The answer keys are organized by unit. The evaluation charts are provided at the end of each unit for you to copy and complete for each child.

SCORING THE TESTS

Answer keys are provided by unit. For Items 1–40, answer keys provide letter answers for the multiple-choice items and sample answers for the constructed-response items. For the writing sections, the Writing Scoring Rubrics are designed to score any kind of writing. Each rubric has a point scale from 1 to 5. Writing Scoring Rubrics appear with each unit. Sample child responses and scores are also provided per unit. (See the General Directions for Writing Assessment on page *x* of this manual.)

Multiple-choice items: Each multiple-choice item has three unlabeled answer choices with bubbles to fill in. Use the answer key provided for each section and assign 2 points to each correct answer and 0 points to each incorrect answer. You may wish to assign a score of 1 if you give assistance to the child during that section.

Constructed-response items: Use the answer keys and the scoring rubric provided below to help score constructed-response items. Award each constructed-response answer a score from 0–2 depending upon how complete the answer is.

Points	Description
2	The response indicates a full understanding of the question's reading or critical thinking skill. The response is accurate and complete. Necessary support and/or examples are included, and the information is clearly text-based.
1	The response indicates a partial understanding of the question's reading or critical thinking skill. The response includes information that is essentially correct and text-based, but it is too general or too simplistic. Some of the support and/or examples may be incomplete or omitted.
0	The response is inaccurate, confused, and/or irrelevant, or the child has failed to respond to the task.

ABOUT INTERPRETATION

This manual provides brief explanations of the possible reasoning behind children's selection of specific answers to the test items. Such information may help in identifying the specific difficulties an English learner may have when navigating a text and processing and decoding information presented in written form. The rationales provided for each item are intended to guide the teachers in applying the concepts assessed in a broader instructional context. Although no assessment can claim to be comprehensive, when items are clearly measuring a standard, they guide teachers in addressing a child's level of mastery, be it to implement remediation measures or promote the child to a more complex level of instruction.

ABOUT EVALUATION

Use the Unit Evaluation chart to track items correctly, and to record test scores. Make one copy per child. This unit chart will help identify skills for which children may need extra work. To calculate an assessment score out of 100 you may wish to multiply the writing and fluency scores by two so each has a possible value of 10. For Unit R and Unit 1, since these units do not have a fluency assessment, you may wish to multiply the writing score by four so it has a possible value of 20. This will give a possible total of 100 points on the entire Unit Test for every unit.

The chart on the following page can be used to track progress of your class, unit by unit. Copy once and use this chart to record children's scores after each unit test. Looking at overall class progress can provide valuable insights into places where children are improving and/or struggling as a group or if any children stand out.

Grade 1 Progress Monitoring Chart

Teacher__________________ **Class**____________ **Date**____________

Copy and use this chart to track and compare children's progress from unit to unit.

	Unit R		Unit 1		Unit 2			Unit 3			Unit 4			Unit 5		
Child Names	**A***	**B**	**A**	**B**	**A**	**B**	**C**	**A**	**B**	**C**	**A**	**B**	**C**	**A**	**B**	**C**
1.																
2.																
3.																
4.																
5.																
6.																
7.																
8.																
9.																
10.																
11.																
12.																
13.																
14.																
15.																
16.																
17.																
18.																
19.																
20.																

***SCORE A: Skills and Content** **SCORE B: Writing** **SCORE C: Fluency**

General Directions for Writing Assessment

This portion of the test assesses a child's ability to interpret a prompt and respond to it by drawing a picture and writing a few words or sentences. The writing prompts vary by unit, and all prompts refer to the passages in the Comprehension subtests.

ADMINISTERING

Preparation: Make sure children are on the correct page and that they have pencils. You may want to give them scrap paper to use to plan their writing.

Directions: Have children turn to page 22. Read the prompt aloud. Point out the box on page 24 and tell children they will draw in the box. Point out the lines on page 25 and make sure children know that they should write their responses on these lines. You may wish to give children scrap paper to use to plan their writing or tell them to use page 26 as scrap paper.

Read the following to children:
Now we will be doing something different. Turn to page 22 in your test. You are going to draw a picture and write about your picture.

Read the prompt to children. Then point out the picture on page 23 and read the caption.

You may wish to read through the checklist for writers on page 27. Or, read the following:

Here are some things to remember when you are drawing and writing:

- **Plan your picture and sentences before you begin writing.**
- **Begin each sentence with a capital letter.**
- **End each sentence with an end mark.**
- **Make sure your sentences make sense.**
- **Make sure the words are spelled correctly. If you are not sure how to spell a word, sound the word out and spell it as best you can.**
- **Make sure your sentences are the way you want readers to read them.**

Give children 15 to 20 minutes to complete their activity.

SCORING

To evaluate children's responses to a writing prompt, familiarize yourself with the writing prompt and review the Five-Point Scoring Rubric found in each unit section of this Teacher's Manual (example rubric provided below). Use the scoring rubric and the sample responses provided to evaluate individual children's writing by assigning a point value of 1–5. Record the scores on the Unit Test Evaluation Form.

5-Point Scoring Rubric				
5	**4**	**3**	**2**	**1**
• writing is focused on topic • idea is very clear • sentences are complete • excellent use of writing conventions • drawing is related to the topic	• writing is focused on topic • idea is clear • sentences are mostly complete • very good use of writing conventions • drawing is related to the topic	• writing is mostly focused on topic • idea is mostly clear • sentences are mostly complete • very good use of writing conventions • drawing is mostly related to the topic	• writing is generally focused on topic • idea is generally clear • sentences are incomplete • frequent errors in writing conventions • drawing is incomplete	• writing is not focused on topic • idea is unclear • writes only one sentence; incomplete • shows serious errors in writing conventions • drawing is unrelated to topic or absent

General Directions for Oral Reading Fluency Assessment

UNIT	R	1	2	3 WCPM*	4 WCPM	5 WCPM
Grade 1 Fluency Norms	none	none	none	20–35	30–45	40–60

*WCPM = Words Correct Per Minute

The purpose of a fluency test is to measure a child's reading rate, expression, and accuracy.

- Accuracy refers to how well English learners use decoding skills.
- Rate reflects how many words a child can accurately decode in one minute on grade-level text the child has not seen before. This is scored as words correct per minute (WCPM).
- Expressive reading is directly related to comprehension. Fluent readers read with controlling stress, pitch variations, intonation, phrasing, and pausing in their voices. This is scored using a rubric.

This one-minute assessment is administered to children individually. Children should not be given the passage until it is time for the assessment. This portion of the test may be given at any time. It does not need to be administered in the same day as the other parts. The general process will be as follows:

- Use a passage of approximately 100–150 words (grade 1–2) and 150–250 words (grades 3–5) written at the child's grade level placement.
- Ask the child to read the passage for one minute. Tape-record the reading. Emphasize that the text should be read aloud in a normal way.
- Mark any uncorrected errors made by the child, such as mispronunciations, substitutions, reversals, omissions, or words pronounced by the examiner after a wait of two to three seconds without an attempt or response from the child. Mark the end point in the text after one minute of reading.

ADMINISTERING

Give the child a copy of the Student Copy of the passage for the test, and make a copy of the Teacher Copy for yourself, noting the formula for calculation at the bottom of the page. The Teacher Copy has a scale of running numbers to make it easier for you to know how many words the child read during the fluency check, while the passages in the Student Copy do not have the numbers. Make sure you have put the child's name and the test date at the top of your copy of the passage. Have a watch or clock available for timing the reading.

Have the child read the text aloud. Do not have the child read the title as part of the fluency reading; it is not included in the running word count. (You may want to tape-record the child's reading for later evaluation.) Stop the child at exactly one minute and note precisely where the child stopped.

As the child reads orally, on your copy of the text, mark any miscues or errors the child makes during the reading (see the chart included with the sample test). Count the total number of words the child read in a minute. Subtract any words the child read incorrectly. Record the words correct per minute score on the test.

How to Identify Reading Miscues/Errors: The chart below shows the kinds of miscues and errors to look for as a child reads aloud and the notations to use to mark them. If the child hesitates over a word, wait several seconds before telling the child what the word is. If a child makes the same error more than once, count it as only one error. Self-correction is not counted as an actual error. However, writing "SC" over the word or words will help you identify words that give the child some difficulty.

Reading Miscue	Notations
Omission The child omits words or word parts.	Some days are (so) cold!
Substitution The child substitutes words or parts of words for the words in the text.	Bears go to caves *and* ~~to~~ sleep.
Insertion The child inserts words or parts of words that are not in the text.	Small children like to run ^*out* in the cold.
Mispronunciation/Misreading The child pronounces or reads a word incorrectly.	*Came* Cold winds come.
Hesitation The child hesitates over a word and the teacher provides the word.	*H* Children have mittens and hats so they can play outside.
Self-correction The child reads a word incorrectly but then corrects the error.	*SC* Big children like to skate on the ice.

Sample Fluency Passage: Here is the passage marked as shown on the previous chart. As the child reads the passage aloud to you, mark miscues and errors. Have the child read for exactly one minute, and then mark the last word the child reads.

Name *Susan*

Wind and Ice

Some days are (so) cold! Cold winds *came* come. There is ice. 11
Bears go to caves *and* ~~to~~ sleep. *H* Children have mittens and hats so 23
they can play outside. Small children like to run ^*out* in the cold. 35
Big children like to *SC* skate on the / ice. They all ride on sleds. 48
They slide down the white hills. Cold days are fun! 58

42 - 5 = 37

SCORING

Determining WCPM: Using the line word counts, add the total number of words read, subtract the errors, and record the number of words the child read correctly in the box labeled "Fluency Score" in the bottom right-hand corner of the page.

Note: Errors include: 1) words read incorrectly; 2) words left out or inserted; 3) mispronounced words; 4) dropped endings or sounds; and 5) reversals (each reversal is counted as one error). Self-corrections and word repetitions are not marked as errors.

Assessing Expression: Rubrics are usually used to assess expression. You can listen to a child read for 1 minute (60 seconds) and assess his or her general reading proficiency and fluency through a scale such as the one suggested below:

Score	Descriptions
5	• reads mostly in large, meaningful phrase groups • has occasional (one/two per paragraph) regressions, repetitions, and deviations from text • demonstrates consistent skill in expressive interpretation • reads at a rate appropriate to grade level placement
4	• uses primarily three- and four-word phrase groups • maintains the original syntax, and phrasing is appropriate and preserves the syntax of the author • demonstrates limited or no expressive interpretation skill • generally reads at a rate appropriate to grade level placement
3	• reads primarily in two-word phrase groups • occasionally reads word-by-word (at least twice per paragraph) • does not demonstrate understanding of word groupings and reading is awkward and unrelated to the larger context of the text • reads most sections of the text at rates that are excessively slow or fast
2	• reads primarily word-by-word • demonstrates no skill for expressive interpretation (tone is flat, no syllabication or stress patterns evident, punctuation marks are ignored) • reads text excessively slowly or with excessive speed
1	• reads producing truncated sounds, disregarding letter-sound correspondence • uses flat tone, no syllabication or stress pattern evident • stops frequently as he/she tries to sound out words letter by letter

INTERPRETING RESULTS

On the Unit Test Evaluation Chart, enter the fluency score for words correct per minute (WCPM). Then enter the Expression score from the rubric. Both numbers can be used to assess children's progress in fluency unit by unit. Improvement in fluency may occur as exposure to models of fluent oral readings in English increases. In addition, reading more material at individual ability levels will lead to increased fluency in English.

To help children improve fluency scores, use notes on miscues to analyze errors and help determine where to focus instruction and remediation. *Does the child make errors that indicate his or her decoding skills are poor?* If so, further instruction in phonics may be needed. *Do the errors reflect a lack of comprehension or limited vocabulary?* In that case, instruction in comprehension strategies and exposure to more vocabulary words may help.

Grade 1, Readiness Unit
Answer Key and Directions

COMPREHENSION: (Recommended Time: 30–45 minutes, uninterrupted)

Teacher Directions: Directions in **bold** are to be read aloud; others are for your information only. Use the following directions to administer the assessment. Make sure all children have a test booklet copy and pencils, and that children are on page 2 of the booklet.

Explain that they will listen to a story and then answer some questions about it. Have children look at the picture and follow along as you read. Be sure to pause after each question so that children have time to mark their answers.

Read the following to the children:

Now I am going to read a story about a boy named Dan and his family. After the first part of the story, I will ask you some questions. Listen carefully. The story is called "Dan and Baby Sam." Here is the first part of the story.

Dan and Baby Sam

1 **Today was the big day!**

2 **Grandpa was coming to Dan's house.**

3 **He wants to see Dan's new baby brother, Sam.**

Now look at page 3.

4 **Dan was very happy.**

5 **He hoped Grandpa would read him a story.**

6 **He hoped they would play with Dan's trains.**

Now turn to page 4.

7 **Grandpa gave Dan a big hug.**

8 **Then he went to see Baby Sam.**

9 **Grandpa did not play with Dan.**

10 **Dan was very sad.**

Now model how to fill in the answer circles. Demonstrate the directions to the children, using a student test book. Read each question twice.

Tell the children:

Now look at page 5. I am going to ask you some questions about this part of the story. For each question that I ask, you will see three pictures in a row. Ask yourself which picture goes with the question I ask. Fill in the circle below the picture that shows the best answer. Listen carefully.

(Comprehension continued)

1. **Look at the first row of pictures at the top of the page. Who is Dan? Is he *a baby . . . a boy . . .* or *an older man*? Put your finger on the picture that shows who Dan is. Then fill in the circle next to the picture you chose.**
2. **Point to the next row of pictures. Which shows how Dan felt before Grandpa came to visit? Was he *happy . . . mad . . .* or *sad*? Fill in the circle below the picture that shows the best answer.**
3. **Move down to the next row of pictures. What did Dan want to do with Grandpa? Did he want to *go swimming . . . paint a picture . . .* or *play trains* with Grandpa? Fill in the circle below the picture that shows the best answer.**

Now turn to page 6.

4. **Look at the top row of pictures. Who did Grandpa play with instead? Was it *Sam . . . Dan . . .* or a *dog?* Fill in the circle below the picture that shows the best answer.**
5. **Look down at the next row of pictures. Which shows how Dan felt at the end of this part of the story? Was he *happy . . . mad . . .* or *sad*? Fill in the circle below the picture that shows the best answer.**

Look at page 7. Now I am going to read the second part of the story. Then I will ask you some more questions. Listen carefully. Here is the rest of the story.

Dan and Baby Sam (part 2)

11 **Grandpa played with Baby Sam.**

12 **Dan sat in his room all alone.**

13 **Dan was very sad.**

14 **"Dan, what is wrong?" Grandpa asked.**

Now turn to page 8.

15 **"No one will play with me," said Dan.**

16 **"Come with me," said Grandpa.**

17 **Dan did.**

18 **"I will read a story to you and Sam," Grandpa said.**

19 **Dan liked to read with Grandpa and Sam.**

Now the story about Dan and his family is over, and I will ask you more questions. Look at page 9.

6. **Look at the first row of pictures. Who is Sam? Is Sam a *baby . . . a boy . . .* or *an older man?* Put your finger on the picture that shows who Sam is. Then fill in the circle below that picture.**

(Comprehension continued)

7. **Move down to the next row of pictures. What did Grandpa do with Dan and Sam? Did he *build with blocks . . . read a book . . .* or *have a picnic?* Fill in the circle below the picture that shows what Grandpa did with Dan and Sam.**

8. **Point to the next row of pictures. Which shows how Dan felt at the end of the story? Was he *happy . . . mad . . .* or *sad*? Fill in the circle below the picture you chose.**

Now turn to page 10.

9. **Look at the first row of pictures. Where does part of this story take place? Put your finger on the picture that shows where this story takes place. Did it take place *at the park . . . at Dan's school . . .* or *in Dan's room*? Fill in the circle below the picture you chose.**

10. **Look at the next row of pictures. What was the end of the story about? Did the story end with *Dan building a snowman . . . Dan fishing . . .* or *Dan reading a story with Grandpa and Baby Sam?* Put your finger on the picture that shows how this story ends. Fill in the circle below the picture you chose.**

<u>**Scoring:**</u> Photocopy and use the evaluation charts to track children's scores and progress.

<u>**Comprehension Answer Key with Interpretation:**</u>

1. Who is Dan?

○ ● ○

Children may have chosen the first picture because the baby is another character in the story.

Correct response: second picture

Children may have chosen the third picture because they did not listen carefully.

(Comprehension continued)

2. Which shows how Dan felt before Grandpa came to visit?

Correct response: first picture

Children may have chosen the second picture because they did not listen to the details of the story.

Children may have chosen the third picture because they did not listen to the details of the story.

3. What did Dan want to do with Grandpa?

Children may have chosen the first picture because they did not listen to the plot of the story.

Children may have chosen the second picture because they did not listen to the plot of the story.

Correct response: third picture

4. Who did Grandpa play with instead?

Correct response: first picture

Children may have chosen the second picture because they confused the boy and baby.

Children may have chosen the third picture because they did not listen carefully to the story.

(Comprehension continued)

5. Which shows how Dan felt at the end of this part of the story?

Children may have chosen the first picture if they were thinking about the beginning of the story.

Children may not be able to distinguish facial expressions for mad and sad in the second picture.

Correct response: third picture

6. Who is Sam?

Correct response: first picture

Children may have chosen the second picture because a boy is another character in the story.

Children may have chosen the third picture because a grandfather is another character in the story.

7. What did Grandpa do with Dan and Sam?

Children may have chosen the first picture because they could not recall events from the story.

Correct response: second picture

Children may have chosen the third picture because they could not recall events from the story.

(Comprehension continued)

8. Which shows how Dan felt at the end of the story?

Correct response: first picture

Children may not be able to distinguish facial expressions for mad and sad in the second picture.

Children may have chosen the third picture because they were thinking of how Dan felt earlier in the story.

9. Where does part of this story take place?

Children may have chosen the first picture because they could not recall the setting of the story.

Children may have chosen the second picture because they could not recall the setting of the story.

Correct response: third picture

10. What was the end of the story about?

Children may have chosen the first picture because they could not recall events from the story.

Children may have chosen the second picture because they could not recall events from the story.

Correct response: third picture

(Comprehension continued)

<u>Suggested Remediation</u>: Discuss each part of the story, using the pictures and words to identify the main ideas and details. Review different types of emotions. Help children retell the setting, characters, and plot of the story in their own words.

CHECKING SKILLS (Recommended Time: 20 minutes, uninterrupted)

<u>Teacher Directions:</u> Use the following directions to administer the assessment. Read the sentences aloud more than once if needed. Be sure to pause after each question so that children have time to mark their answers. Make sure all children are on page 11 before you begin.

Read the following to children:

Now I am going to read some sentences to you. The sentences I will read tell about the story "Dan and Baby Sam." Pick the picture that goes with what I read. Listen carefully.

11. Look at the pictures at the top of the page. Here is the sentence: *Dan was very happy*. Which picture shows that Dan felt very happy? Point to that picture. Fill in the circle below the picture you pick.

12. Put your finger next to the second set of pictures. Look at those three pictures. Here is the sentence: *Dan sat in his room all alone*. Find the picture that shows Dan sitting in his room all alone. Fill in the circle below that picture.

13. Look at the next row of pictures. Here is the sentence: *Grandpa played with Baby Sam.* Find the picture that shows Grandpa playing with Baby Sam. Point to that picture. Fill in the circle below the picture.

Now turn to page 12.

14. Put your finger next to the first row of pictures. Here is the sentence: *Dan was very sad.* Which picture shows that Dan felt very sad? Fill in the circle below that picture.

15. Now look at the last row of pictures on this page. Here is the sentence: *Dan liked reading with Grandpa and Baby Sam.* Which picture shows that Dan liked to read with Grandpa and Baby Sam? Fill in the circle below that picture.

Look at page 13. Now I am going to read to you. Follow along in your book while I read aloud. I will ask you something about each sentence. You can write your answers on the lines.

16. Dan sat in his room.

Write the noun that names a place.

17. The baby smiled.

Write the noun in the sentence.

(Checking Skills continued)

18. Grandpa played with Baby Sam.

Write the verb in this sentence.

Now turn to page 14.

I am going to read part of a sentence. You need to finish the sentence. I will tell you what kind of word to write.

19. Grandpa was coming to Dan's . . .

Write the word that tells about the story's setting.

20. Dan was very . . .

Write the word that tells how Dan felt at the end of the story.

Scoring: Photocopy and use the evaluation chart to track children's scores and progress.

Checking Skills Answer Key with Interpretation:

11. **Dan was very happy.**

Correct response: first picture

Children may have chosen the second picture because they are unable to relate an emotion to a picture.

Children may have chosen the third picture because they are unable to relate an emotion to a picture.

12. **Dan sat in his room all alone.**

Children may have chosen the first picture because they did not understand *his room* to mean *bedroom.*

Children may have chosen the second picture because they did not understand *his room* to mean *bedroom.*

Correct response: third picture

(Checking Skills continued)

13. **Grandpa played with Baby Sam.**

Children may have chosen the first picture because they misunderstood how a baby and a grandpa can play together.

Correct response: second picture

Children may have chosen the third picture because they misunderstood how a baby and a grandpa can play together.

14. **Dan was very sad.**

Children may have chosen the first picture because they are unable to relate an emotion to a picture.

Children may have chosen the second picture because they are unable to relate an emotion to a picture.

Correct response: third picture

15. **Dan liked reading with Grandpa and Baby Sam.**

Correct response: first picture

Children may have chosen the second picture because they misunderstood what Dan liked to do.

Children may have chosen the third picture because they misunderstood what Dan liked to do.

(Checking Skills continued)

Constructed-response Items

16. Correct response: *room*

    Children may have written *Dan* because the word is a proper noun that names a person. Children may have written other words that they heard because they do not know types of words in sentences.

17. Correct response: *baby*

    Children may not understand that *baby* can be a noun that names a person even if the word is not a name. Children may have written *the* or *smiled* because they wrote any word they could remember.

18. Correct response: *played*

    Children may not understand what a verb is.

19. Correct response: *house*

    Children may have written another word because they do not understand the setting of the story.

20. Correct response: *happy*

    Children may have been confused with the different emotions that Dan experiences in the story and written *sad*.

Suggested Remediation: Work with children to review nouns for people, places, and things. Define nouns, verbs, and adjectives, giving examples of each. Have them name objects in the classroom and then describe the object and how a person could use the object. Review the parts of a story, including characters, setting, and plot.

WORD ANALYSIS: (Recommended Time: 20–30 minutes, uninterrupted)

Teacher Directions: Have children turn to page 15. Use the following directions to administer the assessment. Read the words and sentences aloud, more than once if needed. Be sure to pause after each question so that children have time to mark their answers.

Read the following directions to children:

Now we are going to match the pictures to the words on the page. Listen carefully. You will decide which word goes with the picture.

21. Put your finger on the first picture on the page. What do you see in the picture? Next, look at the three words. Does the picture show *a vet . . . a man . . .* or *a van?* Fill in the circle next to the word you chose.

22. Look at the second picture. Which word does the picture show: *run . . . bun* . . . or *ram?* Fill in the circle next to the word you chose.

(Word Analysis continued)

23. Point to the third picture. What does it show? Does the picture show *a cap . . . a cat. . . .* or *a can?* Fill in the circle next to the word you chose.

Turn to page 16. Now you are going to choose sentences that match the picture. As before, look at the pictures and the words as you decide. Pick the complete sentence.

24. Put your finger on the next picture. How would we correctly say what is happening? Is it *Dogs like dig . . . The dog likes to dig . . .* or *The dog likes?* Fill in the circle next to the sentence you chose.

25. Move down to the next picture. Which sentence correctly tells about what the picture shows? Would we say *This is my map . . . These maps me* . . . or *The map is four?*

Look at page 17. Now we will study words. This time you will decide what the beginning letter sound is for each word. Then you will choose a word that makes the same beginning letter sound.

26. The word is *fan.* Now, which of the three words starts with the same letter as *fan*? Is it *pan . . . fun . . .* or *mat*? Fill in the circle next to the word you chose.

27. The word is *sit.* Now, which of the three words starts with the same letter as *sit?* Is it *sail . . . mitt . . .* or *pats?* Fill in the circle next to the word you chose.

Now turn to page 18.

28. The word is *bat.* Now, which of the three words starts with the same letter as *bat?* Is it *ball . . . web . . .* or *mat*? Fill in the circle below the word you chose.

29. The word is *pot.* Now, which of the three words starts with the same letter as *pot?* Is it *lap . . . hot . . .* or *pet*? Fill in the circle below the word you chose.

30. The word is *lion.* Now, which of the three words starts with the same letter as *lion?* Is it *pail . . . lap . . .* or *real?* Fill in the circle below the word you chose.

<u>Scoring:</u> Photocopy and use the evaluation chart to track children's scores and progress.

(**Word Analysis continued**)

Word Analysis Answer Key with Interpretation:

21. **Correct response:** *van*

    Children may have chosen *vet* because they heard the initial /v/.

    Children may have chosen *man* because they heard the rhyming part.

22. **Correct response:** *run*

    Children may have chosen *bun* because they heard the rhyming part.

    Children may have chosen *ram* because they heard the initial /r/.

23. **Correct response:** *can*

    Children may have chosen either *cat* or *cap* because they heard the initial /k/.

24. **Correct response:** *The dog likes to dig.*

    Children may have chosen *Dogs like dig* because they heard the words in the sentence but not the correct forms.

    Children may have chosen *The dog likes* because they heard the correct start of the sentence but not the ending.

25. **Correct response:** *This is my map.*

    Children may have chosen *These maps me* because the picture shows a map.

    Children my have chosen *The map is four* because the map is folded four times.

26. **Correct response:** *fun*

    Children who chose other responses (*pan, mat*) might not understand the initial letter sound or might have thought they were matching vowel sounds.

27. **Correct response:** *sail*

    Children who chose other responses (*mitt, pats*) might not understand the initial letter sound.

28. **Correct response:** *ball*

    Children who chose other responses (*web, mat*) might not understand the initial letter sound or might confuse other sounds in the words.

29. **Correct response:** *pet*

    Children who chose other responses (*lap, hot*) might not understand the initial letter sound or might confuse other sounds in the words.

30. **Correct response:** *lap*

    Children who chose other responses *(pail, real)* may not understand the initial letter sounds or might confuse other sounds in the words.

(Word Analysis continued)

Suggested Remediation: Review the sound-spellings for *Mm, Cc, Ff, Dd, Rr, Vv, Ss, Pp, Ll,* and *Bb.* Say pairs of words that begin with the same sound. Have children identify the sound and the letter. Then say pairs of words that begin with different sounds. Have children identify each sound and each letter.

VOCABULARY (Recommended Time: 20–30 minutes, uninterrupted)

Teacher Directions: Have children turn to page 19. Use the following directions to administer the assessment.

Read the following directions to children:

Now we will choose pictures that match sentences.

31. Read the sentence: *The children learn in a classroom.* Look at the three pictures. Which picture shows the sentence *The children learn in a classroom?* Fill in the circle below the picture you chose.

32. Read the sentence: *A bird can fly.* Look at the three pictures. Which picture shows the sentence *A bird can fly?* Fill in the circle below the picture you chose.

33. Read the sentence: *The fruit is sweet.* Which picture shows the sentence *The fruit is sweet?* Fill in the circle below the picture you chose.

Turn to page 20.

34. Read the sentence: *I carry a backpack.* Which picture shows the sentence *I carry a backpack?* Fill in the circle below the picture you chose.

35. Read the sentence: *You can buy food.* Which picture shows the sentence *You can buy food?* Fill in the circle below the picture you chose.

Now I will read you questions. You will write the answer. Your answer can be one word. Write the word on the line. Listen carefully.

Be sure to read the questions slowly and, if needed, more than once.

Look at page 21.

36. Look at the picture at the top of the page. *What do you do when you use your eyes to notice something?* Write the word on the line.

37. Put your finger on the next picture. *What do you call a very young child?* Write the word on the line.

38. Look at the next picture. *What is the word for the number 2?* Write the word on the line.

(Vocabulary continued)

39. Move down to the next picture. *What is another word for amusement or enjoyment or having a good time?* Write the word on the line.

40. Put your finger on the last picture. *What do you do when you look at words and understand them?* Write the word on the line.

Scoring: Photocopy and use the evaluation chart to track children's scores and progress.

Vocabulary Answer Key with Interpretation:

31. The children learn in a classroom.

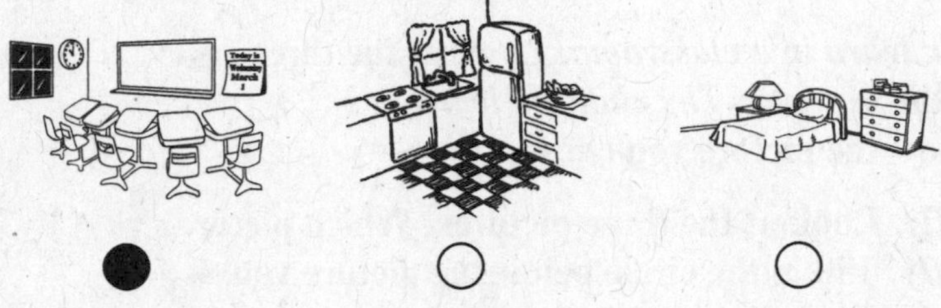

Correct response: first picture

Children may have chosen the second picture because they are unable to define *classroom* using context clues.

Children may have chosen the third picture because they are unable to define *classroom* using context clues.

32. A bird can fly.

Children may not distinguish among things that can fly in the first picture.

Children may not distinguish among things that can fly in the second picture.

Correct response: third picture

(Vocabulary continued)

33. The fruit is sweet.

Children may have chosen the first picture because they are uncertain what fruit looks like.

Correct response: second picture

Children may have chosen the third picture because they are uncertain what fruit looks like.

34. I carry a backpack.

Children may not distinguish among things that can carry other things in the first picture.

Children may not distinguish among things that can carry other things in the second picture.

Correct response: third picture

35. You can buy food.

Correct response: first picture

Children may have chosen the second picture because they are unsure what buying food looks like.

Children may have chosen the third picture because they are unsure what buying food looks like.

(Vocabulary continued)

36. **Correct response:** *see*

    The correct answer is the vocabulary word *see*. If children write another word, such as *look*, they understand the concept and intent of the question but are not using a word they have learned. If children write a word that does not make sense as an answer to the question, they may not understand some of the words in the definition.

37. **Correct response:** *baby*

    The correct answer is the vocabulary word *baby.* If children write another word, such as *kid* or *child*, they understand the concept and intent of the question but are not using a word they have learned. If children write a word that does not make sense as an answer to the question, they may not understand some of the words in the definition.

38. **Correct response:** *two*

    The correct answer is the vocabulary word *two.* If children write the numeral 2, they understand the concept and intent of the question but are not using a word they have learned. If children write a word that does not make sense as an answer to the question, they may not understand some of the words in the definition.

39. **Correct response:** *fun*

    The correct answer is the vocabulary word *fun*. If children write another word, such as *enjoy* or *like*, they understand the concept and intent of the question but are not using a word they have learned. If children write a word that does not make sense as an answer to the question, they may not understand some of the words in the definition. Children may write a word that tells a specific thing that is fun, such as *bike* or *game*. Remind children that the answers to these questions are vocabulary words that have been taught throughout the unit.

40. **Correct response:** *read*

    Children may write *reading* instead of *read.* Encourage them to use the form of the word that they have learned. If children write another word, such as *learn*, they understand the concept and the intent of the question but are not using a word they have learned. If children respond with another vocabulary word such as *see*, remind them to listen to the entire question. If children write a word that does not make sense as an answer to the question, they may not understand some of the words in the definition.

Suggested Remediation: Review the multiple-choice sentences. Discuss all the information provided in the sentences. Then help children identify the answer that best fits the information. Review the unit's vocabulary with children. Use word and definition cards. Have children draw a picture on the word card to help with identification. Then have children match the word cards with their definition cards.

WRITING (Recommended Time: 15–20 minutes, uninterrupted)

Teacher Directions: Have children turn to page 22. Make sure they have pencils. Read the prompt aloud and point out the illustration on page 23. Make sure children know to draw their picture on page 24 and write their response on page 25. Then read through the writing checklist on page 27. You may wish to give children scrap paper to use to plan their writing or permit them to use page 26 as scrap paper.

Read the following directions to children:

For the last part of the test, you will draw a picture and write two sentences about a topic I'm about to read to you. The topic explains what you are going to draw and write about. The topic also gives you some ideas for planning.

If you do not know how to spell a word, sound out the word and do the best you can. Write as neatly as you can. Be sure your sentences are about the topic. Here is the topic you should write about:

Prompt:

In "Dan and Baby Sam," Dan is excited to play with his Grandpa. Think of something you like to do with a member of your family. Who do you like to play with? What do you do? Draw a picture of the family member and the activity. Then write two complete sentences.

Point out the picture of Dan with his Grandpa on page 23. Read the caption: **Here is Dan reading with Grandpa.** Point out the drawing box on page 24 and the lines on page 25 for writing.

Then point out the checklist on page 27. Read the following directions to children.

Here are some things to remember when you are writing:
Did you draw a picture of the family member and the activity?
Did you think about what you like to do with someone in your family?
Did you tell about what you like to do with that person?
Do your sentences make sense?
Do your sentences begin with a capital letter?
Do your sentences end with a punctuation mark?
Remember to look at your drawing.
Remember to write two complete sentences.
Remember to reread your sentences.

Now think about what you would like to draw and write. You have twenty minutes. Remember to ask yourself the questions on page 27 after you are finished working. Make sure you have two complete sentences.

Be sure to answer any questions children may have. Read the prompt a second time. Alert them when they have five minutes remaining.

Scoring: See page xi of this manual for information on how to score Writing.

(Writing continued)

5-Point Scoring Rubric

5	4	3	2	1
• writing is focused on the topic	• writing is focused on topic	• writing is mostly focused on topic	• writing is generally focused on topic	• writing is not focused on topic
• idea is very clear	• idea is clear	• idea is mostly clear	• idea is generally clear	• idea is unclear
• sentences are complete	• sentences are mostly complete	• sentences are mostly complete	• sentences are incomplete	• writes only one sentence; incomplete
• excellent use of writing conventions	• very good use of writing conventions	• good use of writing conventions	• frequent errors in writing conventions	• shows serious errors in writing conventions

Sample Responses:

Possible response (5-point score):

I play games with my mom. We make noise.

Possible response (4-point score):

My brother play ball. It is fun.

Possible response (3-point score):

My dad and me cook. We eat.

Possible response (2-point score):

My sister read.

Possible response (1-point score):

read, play, or other one-word answers

Readiness Unit Test Evaluation Chart

Name ______________________________ **Date** ______________

Item	Skill	Week/Day	Item/Type*	Assistance (circle)	Score (circle one)
1	Character	Week 1 Day 3	MC	Y N	0 1 2
2	Character	Week 1 Day 3	MC	Y N	0 1 2
3	Plot	Week 3 Day 3	MC	Y N	0 1 2
4	Plot	Week 3 Day 3	MC	Y N	0 1 2
5	Character	Week 1 Day 3	MC	Y N	0 1 2
6	Character	Week 1 Day 3	MC	Y N	0 1 2
7	Plot	Week 3 Day 3	MC	Y N	0 1 2
8	Character	Week 1 Day 3	MC	Y N	0 1 2
9	Setting	Week 3 Day 3	MC	Y N	0 1 2
10	Plot	Week 2 Day 3	MC	Y N	0 1 2
11	Character	Week 1 Day 3	MC	Y N	0 1 2
12	Setting	Week 2 Day 3	MC	Y N	0 1 2
13	Character and Plot	Week 1 Day 3 Week 3 Day 3	MC	Y N	0 1 2
14	Character	Week 1 Day 3	MC	Y N	0 1 2
15	Character	Week 1 Day 3	MC	Y N	0 1 2
16	Nouns for Places	Week 2 Day 4	CR	Y N	0 1 2
17	Nouns for People	Week 1 Day 4	CR	Y N	0 1 2
18	Verbs	Week 3 Day 4	CR	Y N	0 1 2
19	Nouns for Things	Week 1 Day 4	CR	Y N	0 1 2
20	Adjectives	Week 5 Day 4	CR	Y N	0 1 2
21	/v/ spelled *Vv*	Week 6 Day 2	MC	Y N	0 1 2
22	/r/ spelled *Rr*	Week 5 Day 2	MC	Y N	0 1 2
23	/k/ spelled *Cc*	Week 2 Day 2	MC	Y N	0 1 2
24	/d/ spelled *Dd*	Week 4 Day 2 Week 6 Day 4	MC	Y N	0 1 2
25	/m/ spelled *Mm*	Week 1 Day 4 Week 6 Day 4	MC	Y N	0 1 2
26	/f/ spelled *Ff*	Week 3 Day 2	MC	Y N	0 1 2
27	/s/ spelled *Ss*	Week 1 Day 2	MC	Y N	0 1 2
28	/b/ spelled *Bb*	Week 3 Day 2	MC	Y N	0 1 2
29	/p/ spelled *Pp*	Week 2 Day 2	MC	Y N	0 1 2
30	/l/ spelled *Ll*	Week 4 Day 2	MC	Y N	0 1 2
31	Vocabulary Words	Week 5 Day 1	MC	Y N	0 1 2
32	Vocabulary Words	Week 5 Day 1	MC	Y N	0 1 2
33	Vocabulary Words	Week 3 Day 1	MC	Y N	0 1 2
34	Vocabulary Words	Week 6 Day 1	MC	Y N	0 1 2
35	Vocabulary Words	Week 6 Day 1	MC	Y N	0 1 2
36	Vocabulary Words	Week 1 Day 1	CR	Y N	0 1 2
37	Vocabulary Words	Week 2 Day 1	CR	Y N	0 1 2
38	Vocabulary Words	Week 4 Day 1	CR	Y N	0 1 2
39	Vocabulary Words	Week 3 Day 1	CR	Y N	0 1 2
40	Vocabulary Words	Week 5 Day 1	CR	Y N	0 1 2
SCORE A: Skills and Content					____ **out of 80**
SCORE B: Writing				Y N	4 8 12 16 20
OVERALL SCORE					____ **out of 100**

***MC = multiple choice CR = constructed response**

Grade 1, Unit 1
Answer Key and Directions

COMPREHENSION (Recommended Time: 30–45 minutes, uninterrupted)

Teacher Directions: Directions in **bold** are to be read aloud; others are for your information only. Use the following directions to administer the assessment. Make sure all children have a test booklet copy and pencils, and that children are on page 2 of the booklet. Explain that they will listen to a story and then answer some questions about it. Have children look at the picture and follow along as you read. Be sure to pause after each question so that children have time to mark their answers.

Read the following to the children:

Now I am going to read a story about a boy and his cat. After the first part of the story, I will ask you some questions. Listen carefully. The story is called "Mittens." Here is the first part of the story.

1 **My name is Matt and I have a pet cat named Mittens.**
2 **One day, Mittens looked sick.**
3 **My mom and I left our apartment and took her to the vet.**

Tell children to look on the next page.

4 **I held Mittens with care and protected her.**
5 **We drove through the city.**

Tell children to turn to page 4.

6 **When we got to the doctor, the vet examined Mittens and smiled.**
7 **He told me that my cat was not sick.**
8 **Mittens was about to have kittens!**

Now model how to fill in the circle. Demonstrate the directions to the children, using a student test book. Read each question twice.

Tell children:

Now look at page 5. I am going to ask you some questions about this part of the story. For each question that I ask, you will see three pictures in a row. Ask yourself which picture goes with the question I ask. Fill in the circle below the picture that shows the best answer. Listen carefully.

1. **Look at the first row of pictures at the top of the page. Where does Matt live? Does he live *in a house* . . . *an apartment building* . . . or *a farm*? Put your finger on the picture that shows where Matt lives. Then fill in the circle below the picture you chose.**

2. **Point to the next row of pictures. Who is Mittens? Is Mittens *a cat* . . . *a boy* . . . or *a boy's mom?* Fill in the circle below the picture that shows the best answer.**

(Comprehension continued)

3. **Move down to the next row of pictures. What animal is very different from Mittens? Is it *a cat . . . a kitten . . .* or *a dog* that is not at all like Mittens?**

Ask children to turn to page 6.

4. **Look at the top row of pictures. Why did Matt take Mittens to the vet? Was it *because Mittens felt sick . . . because Mittens wanted to play . . .* or *because Mittens wanted to chase birds?* Fill in the circle below the picture that shows the best answer.**

5. **Look down at the next row of pictures. What is the story about so far? Is the story about *a girl walking her dog . . . a boy with a sick cat . . .* or *a boy with a fish tank?* Fill in the circle below the picture that shows the best answer.**

Look at page 7. Now I am going to read the second part of the story. Then I will ask you some more questions. Listen carefully. Here is the rest of the story.

"Mittens" (part 2)

9 **When the five little kittens were born, I saw how small they were.**
10 **The kittens slept and drank all day in our apartment.**
11 **A basket kept the kittens safe and warm.**

Now turn to page 8.

12 **Mom told me I could pick one to keep.**
13 **I tied a blue ribbon around my favorite kitten.**
14 **I named my kitten Tiger.**
15 **The rest of Mittens' kittens now live with other girls and boys.**
16 **I thank Mittens for letting me be part of her kitten family!**

Now the story about Mittens is over and I will ask you more questions. Look at page 9.

6. **Look at the first row of pictures. Who is Tiger? Is Tiger *a boy . . . a kitten with stripes . . . or a dog*?** Put your finger on the picture that shows who Tiger is. Then fill in the circle below that picture.

7. **Move down to the next row of pictures. Where did the kittens live after they were born? Did the kittens live *at the zoo . . . on a farm . . .* or *in a room in an apartment?* Fill in the circle below the picture that shows where the kittens lived.**

8. **Point to the next row of pictures. What animal is like Mittens? Is Mittens like *a rabbit . . . hamsters . . .* or *a kitten?* Fill in the circle below the picture you chose.**

Ask children to turn to page 10.

(Comprehension continued)

9. Look at the first row of pictures. How did Matt show which kitten he wanted to keep? Put your finger on the picture that shows how Matt showed which kitten he wanted to keep. Did Matt *play with a dog . . . give the kitten food . . .* or *tie a ribbon on the kitten?* Fill in the circle below the picture that you chose.

10. Look at the next row of pictures. What was the end of the story about? Did the story end with *a boy hugging a kitten . . . a boy with a bunny . . .* or *a boy with a dog?* Put your finger on the picture that shows how the story ends. Fill in the circle below the picture you chose.

Scoring: Photocopy and use the evaluation chart to track children's scores and progress.

Comprehension Answer Key with Interpretation:

1. Where does Matt live?

Children who chose the first picture (a house) may not distinguish between an apartment building and a house.

Correct answer: second picture (an apartment building)

Children who chose the third picture (a farm) may not distinguish between an apartment building and a farm.

2. Who is Mittens?

Correct answer: first picture (black cat with white paws)

Children who chose the second picture (a boy, Matt) may have thought the question was asking about the person who owned or took care of Mittens.

Children who chose the third picture (Matt's mom) may have thought the question was asking about the person who owned or took care of Mittens.

(Comprehension continued)

3. What animal is different from Mittens?

Children who chose the first picture (a cat) may have thought the question was asking what animal is like Mittens.

Children who chose the second picture (a kitten) may have thought the question was asking what animal is like Mittens.

Correct answer: third picture (a dog)

4. Why did Matt take Mittens to the vet?

Correct answer: first picture (black cat with white paws lying on couch looking sick)

Children may have chosen the second picture (cat playing with yarn) because most cats play with yarn.

Children may have chosen the third picture (cat chasing bird) because cats can chase birds.

5. What is the story about so far?

Children may have chosen the first picture (girl walking a dog) because a girl could have a pet dog in another story.

Correct answer: second picture (Matt holding Mittens)

Children may have chosen the third picture (Matt next to a fish tank) because a boy could have pet fish in another story.

(Comprehension continued)

6. Who is Tiger?

Children who chose the first picture (Matt) may have thought the question was asking about the person who owned or took care of Tiger.

Correct answer: second picture (Tiger)

Children who chose the third picture (a dog) may have chosen this item because a dog could be named Tiger.

7. Where did the kittens live after they were born?

Children may have chosen the first picture (a zoo) because kittens could live in a zoo.

Children may have chosen the second picture (a farm) because kittens could live on a farm.

Correct answer: third picture (five kittens by a couch in an apartment setting)

8. What animal is like Mittens?

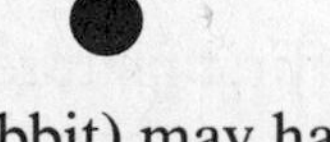

Children who chose the first picture (a rabbit) may have thought the question was asking what animal is different from Mittens.

Children who chose the second picture (hamsters) may have thought the question was asking what animal is different from Mittens.

Correct answer: third picture (kitten)

(Comprehension continued)

9. How did Matt show which kitten he wanted to keep?

○ ○ ●

Children may have chosen the first picture (boy playing fetch with a dog) because a boy could be playing fetch with a dog in another story.

Children may have chosen the second picture (boy holding a food bowl for a kitten) because Matt would need to feed the kitten he keeps.

Correct answer: third picture (boy tying ribbon on kitten)

10. What was the end of the story about?

● ○ ○

Correct answer: first picture (boy hugging a striped kitten)

Children may have chosen the second picture (boy with bunny) because a bunny could be a boy's pet.

Children may have chosen the third picture (boy with dog) because a dog could be a boy's pet.

Suggested Remediation: Discuss each part of the story, using the pictures and words to identify the main ideas. Have children compare and contrast animals to Mittens. Give examples of causes from the story and have children tell about their effects. Help children retell the setting, characters, and plot in their own words.

CHECKING SKILLS (Recommended Time: 20 minutes, uninterrupted)

Teacher Directions: Use the following directions to administer the assessment. Read the sentences aloud more than once if needed. Be sure to pause after each question so that children have time to mark their answers. Make sure all children are on page 11 before you begin.

Read the following to children:

Now I am going to read some sentences to you. The sentences I will read tell about the story "Mittens." Pick the picture that goes with what I read. Listen carefully.

11. **Look at the pictures at the top of the page. Here is the sentence: *My name is Matt and I have a cat named Mittens.* Which picture shows that Matt has a cat named Mittens? Point to that picture. Fill in the circle below the picture you pick.**
12. **Put your finger next to the second row of pictures. Look at those three pictures. Here is the sentence: *One day, Mittens looked sick.* Find the picture that shows that Mittens looked sick. Fill in the circle below that picture.**
13. **Look at the next row of pictures. Here is the sentence: *He told me my cat was not sick.* Find the picture that shows a vet telling Matt his cat was not sick. Point to that picture. Fill in the circle below the picture.**

Tell children:

Now turn to page 12.

14. **Put your finger next to the next row of pictures. Here is the sentence: *A basket kept the kittens safe and warm.* Which picture shows a basket keeping kittens safe and warm? Fill in the circle below that picture.**
15. **Now look at the last row of pictures on the page. Here is the sentence: *I tied a blue ribbon around my favorite kitten.* Which picture shows Matt tying a blue ribbon around the kitten? Fill in the circle below that picture.**

Look at page 13. Now I am going to read to you. Follow along in your book while I read aloud. I will ask you one question about each sentence. You can write your answers on the lines.

16. **mittens looked sick.**
    Write the word correctly that should begin with an uppercase letter.
17. **cat small is the**
    Put these words in order to make a statement. Be sure you write a sentence.
18. **The cat went to the vet.**
    Write the predicate in this sentence.

Now turn to page 14.

19. **The dog is ________.**
    Write an adjective to complete this sentence.
20. **Do you have a cat**
    Add the punctuation mark that makes this a question.

(Checking Skills continued)

<u>**Scoring:**</u> Photocopy and use the evaluation chart to track student scores and progress.

<u>**Checking Skills Answer Key with Interpretation:**</u>

11. My name is Matt and I have a cat named Mittens.

Correct answer: first picture (Matt holding Mittens)

Children may have chosen the second picture (girl with a dog) because a girl could have a dog for a pet.

Children may have chosen the third picture (woman with a bird) because a woman could have a bird for a pet.

12. One day, Mittens looked sick.

Children may have chosen the first picture (a dog chasing a cat) because dogs can chase cats.

Children may have chosen the second picture (a cat playing with a bird) because cats like to watch birds.

Correct answer: third picture (cat looking sick)

(**Checking Skills continued**)

13. He told me my cat was not sick.

Children may have chosen the first picture (Matt using thermometer) because the boy is sick in the picture and the sentence mentions sickness.

Correct answer: second picture (a vet holding Mittens)

Children may have chosen the third picture (Mom talking to Matt) because Matt's mom may have talked to him about his cat.

14. A basket kept the kittens safe and warm.

Correct answer: first picture (five kittens in a basket)

Children who chose the second picture (eggs in a basket) may have thought the question was asking what could be put into a basket.

Children who chose the third picture (a picnic basket) may have thought the question was asking what could be put into a basket.

15. I tied a blue ribbon around my favorite kitten.

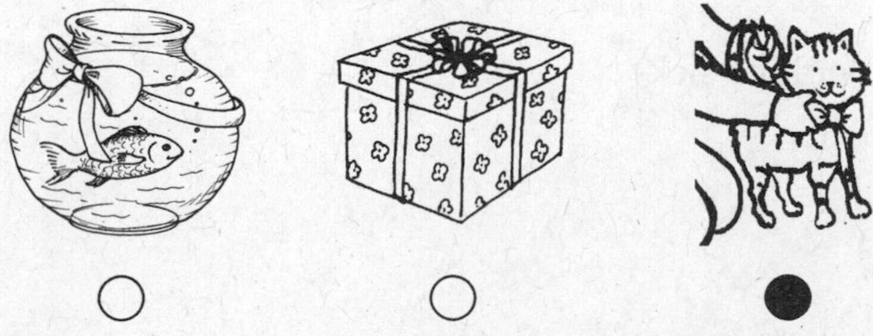

Children who chose the first picture (bow around a fish bowl) may have thought the question was asking what object a bow could be tied around.

Children who chose the second picture (bow on a gift) may have thought the question was asking what object a bow could be tied around.

Correct answer: third picture (Tiger with ribbon on neck)

(Checking Skills continued)

Constructed-response Items

16. **Correct response:** *Mittens*

    Children may not realize that this is a complete sentence since it only contains three words. Children may not capitalize the beginning of sentences or proper nouns.

17. **Correct response:** *The cat is small.*

    Children may rewrite the sentence, "Is the cat small?" Children also may write only one of the words on the line instead of creating a sentence.

18. *went to the vet*

    Children may identify *the cat* as the predicate.

19. **Possible answers:** *cute, furry, small, big, soft, loving*

    Children may not identify an adjective to complete the statement. Children may use a noun or a verb.

20. **Correct response:** *Children should add a question mark after the word* cat.

    Children may not add a question mark to make a question. They may use a period or exclamation point.

Suggested Remediation: Discuss capitalization and punctuation with children. Have children find examples throughout the story. Give children a subject from the story and have them identify the predicate or create their own. Help children find past tense verbs, adjectives, and words ending in *-s* in the story.

WORD ANALYSIS (Recommended Time: 20–30 minutes, uninterrupted)

Teacher Directions: Have children turn to page 15. Use the following directions to administer the assessment. Read the words and sentences aloud more than once if needed. Be sure to pause after each question so that children have time to mark their answers.

Tell children:

Now we are going to match the pictures to the words on the page. Listen carefully. You will decide which word goes with the picture.

21. **Put your finger on the picture at the top of the page. What do you see in the picture? Next look at the three words. Does the picture show *dust . . . a puck* . . . or *a duck?* Fill in the circle under the word you chose.**

22. **Look at the second picture. Does that picture show *a box . . . a fox* . . . or *foam?* Fill in the circle under the word you choose.**

23. **Point to the third picture. What does it show? Does the picture show *pets . . . pans* . . . or *pies?* Fill in the circle under the word you chose.**

(Word Analysis continued)

Turn to page 16. Now you are going to choose sentences that match the pictures. As before, look at the pictures and the words as you decide.

24. Put your finger on the next picture. How would we correctly say what is happening? Is it *I give the cat water . . . The cat climbs trees* . . . or *I am the cat?* Fill in the circle next to the sentence you chose.

25. Move down to the next picture. How would we say what is happening in the picture? Would we say *I help the dog. . . . I like fish* . . . or *I help and love the cat?* Fill in the circle next to the sentence you chose.

Look at page 17. Now we will study words. This time you will decide what vowel sound a word makes. Then you will choose a word that makes the same vowel sound.

26. The word is *cat.* Now, which of the words make the same vowel sound as the word *cat?* Is it *dad . . . lost* . . . or *cake?* Fill in the circle next to the word you chose.

27. The word is *net.* Which word makes the same vowel sound as the word *net?* Is it *meet . . . no* . . . or *vet?* Fill in the circle next to the word you chose.

28. The word is *pig.* Which word makes the same vowel sound as the word *pig?* Is it *peg . . . big* . . . or *pan?* Fill in the circle next to the word you chose.

Now turn to page 18.

29. The word is *top.* Which word makes the same vowel sound as the word *top?* Is it *dot . . . rip* . . . or *cat?* Fill in the circle next to the word you chose.

30. The word is *sun.* Which word makes the same vowel sound as the word *sun*? Is it *sat . . . see* . . . or *fun?* Fill in the circle next to the word you chose.

<u>Scoring</u>: Photocopy and use the evaluation chart to track children's scores and progress.

<u>Word Analysis Answer Key with Interpretation</u>:

21. **Correct response:** *duck*

Children may have chosen *dust* because they thought the directions were to match the beginning sounds.

Children may have chosen *puck* because they thought the directions given were to match word families.

22. **Correct response:** *fox*

Children may have chosen *box* because they thought the directions given were to match word families.

Children may have chosen *foam* because they thought the directions given were to match initial consonants.

(Word Analysis continued)

23. **Correct response:** *pies*

    Children may have chosen *pets* or *pans* because they thought the directions given were to match initial consonants.

24. **Correct answer:** I give the cat water.

    Children may have chosen *The cat climbs trees* because the sentence was not heard correctly or misinterpreted.

    Children may have chosen *I am the cat* because the sentence was not heard correctly or misinterpreted.

25. **Correct answer:** I help and love the cat.

    Children who chose *I help the dog* or *I like fish* may not have heard or may have forgotten the word *cat.*

26. **Correct answer:** *dad*

    Children who gave other responses *(lost, cake)* may not have understood the short vowel sound in *cat.*

27. **Correct answer:** *vet*

    Children who gave other responses *(meet, no)* may not have understood the short vowel sound in *net.*

28. **Correct answer:** *big*

    Children who gave other responses *(peg, pan)* may not have understood the short vowel sound in *pig.*

29. **Correct answer:** *dot*

    Children who gave other responses *(rip, cat)* may not have understood the short vowel sound in *top.*

30. **Correct answer:** *fun*

    Children who gave other responses *(sat, see)* may not have understood the short vowel sound in *sun.*

<u>**Suggested Remediation:**</u> Discuss short vowel sounds with children. Have children find examples throughout the unit selection story. Help children create a list of words containing each vowel sound.

VOCABULARY (Recommended Time: 20–30 minutes, uninterrupted)

Teacher Directions: Have children turn to page 19. Use the following directions to administer the assessment.

Tell children:
Now we will choose pictures that match sentences.

31. Read the sentence *The cat drank from her bowl.* Look at the three pictures. Which picture shows what happens in the sentence *The cat drank from her bowl?* Fill in the circle below the picture you chose.

32. Read the sentence *I take care of my pet.* Look at the three pictures. Which picture shows what happens in the sentence *I take care of my pet?* Fill in the circle below the picture you chose.

33. Read the sentence *The vet examined the dog.* Look at the three pictures. Which picture shows what happens in the sentence *The vet examined the dog?* Fill in the circle below the picture you chose.

Now turn to page 20.

34. Read the sentence *We saw boats on the water.* Look at the three pictures. Which picture shows what happens in the sentence *We saw boats on the water?* Fill in the circle below the picture you chose.

35. Read the sentence *The hiker walked far.* Look at the three pictures. Which picture shows what happens in the sentence *The hiker walked far?* Fill in the circle below the picture you chose.

Look at page 21. Now I will read you questions. You will write the answer. Your answer can be one word. Write the word on the line. Listen carefully.

Be sure to read the questions slowly and, if needed, more than once.

36. Look at the picture at the top of the page. *What type of animal do you see?*

37. Put your finger on the next picture. *What is something that is not dirty?* Write that word on the line.

38. Look at the next picture. *What do you call moving through the air?* Write the word on the line.

39. Move down to the next picture. *What is a large plant with branches, leaves, and a thick trunk?* Write the word on the line.

40. Put your finger on the last picture. *What do you call a group of animals of the same kind?* Write the word on the line.

(Vocabulary continued)

<u>Vocabulary Answer Key with Interpretation:</u>

<u>Scoring</u>: Photocopy and use the evaluation chart to track student scores and progress.

31. The cat **drank** from her bowl.

Children who answered with the first picture (cat playing with yarn) may have identified the word *cat*. They may not have understood the word *drank*.

Correct response: second picture (cat drinking from a bowl)

Children who answered with the third picture (cat sleeping) may have identified the word *cat*. They may not have understood or read the word *drank*.

32. I take care of my **pet**.

Correct answer: first picture (girl giving a dog a bath)

Children who answered with the second picture (man watering a plant) may have identified the word *care*. The man cares for the plant. They may not have understood or read the word *pet*.

Children who answered with the third picture (girl on a bicycle) may have identified the word *love*. The girl loves to ride her bike. They may not have understood or read the word *pet*.

(Vocabulary continued)

33. The vet examined the dog.

● ○ ○

Correct answer: first picture (vet examining dog)

Children who answered with the second picture (boy walking a dog) may have identified the word *dog*. They may not have understood or heard the word *examined.*

Children who answered with the third picture (pet store) may have identified the word *dog* and where the dog could have been purchased. They may not have understood or heard the word *examined.*

34. We saw **boats** on the water.

○ ● ○

Children who answered with the first picture (two children fishing) may have chosen this item because some children like to fish in boats or on the shore.

Correct answer: second picture (three sailboats on the water)

Children who answered with the third picture (fish underwater) may have identified the word *water*.

(Vocabulary continued)

35. The **hiker** walked far.

● ○ ○

Correct answer: first picture (hiker)

Children may have chosen the second picture (boy running) because a boy could begin to run while on a walk.

Children may have chosen the third picture (person on a bike) because children may confuse a hiker with a biker.

36. **Correct response:** *dolphin*

The correct answer is the vocabulary word *dolphin*. If children write another word, such as *fish* or *whale,* they understand the concept and intent of the question but are not using a word they have learned. If children write a word that does not make sense as an answer to the question, they may not understand some of the words in the definition.

37. **Correct response:** *clean*

The correct answer is the vocabulary word *clean*. If children write another word, such as *spotless* or *fresh,* they understand the concept and intent of the question but are not using a word they have learned. Children could possibly respond with a word of something that is clean, like *shirt* or *plate.* Remind children that the answers to these questions are vocabulary words that have been taught throughout the unit.

38. **Correct response:** *flying*

The correct answer is the vocabulary word *flying*. Children may write *fly* instead of *flying*. Encourage children to respond with the form of the word that they learned. If children write another word, such as *soaring,* they understand the concept and intent of the question but are not using a word they have learned. Children could possibly respond with a word explaining an object that moves through the air, such as *kite* or *airplane.* Remind children that the answers to these questions are vocabulary words that have been taught throughout the unit.

39. **Correct response:** *tree*

The correct answer is the vocabulary word *tree*. If children write another word, such as *flower,* they show some understanding of the concept and intent of the question but are not listening carefully to all of the clues in the question. Children could possibly respond with a word explaining a type of tree, such as *maple* or *oak*. Remind children that the answers to these questions are vocabulary words that have been taught throughout the unit.

(Vocabulary continued)

40. **Correct response:** *herd*

The correct answer is the vocabulary word *herd.* If children write another word, such as *flock* or *pack,* they understand the concept and intent of the question but are not using a word they have learned. Children could possibly respond with a word naming a group of animals, such as *cattle.* Remind children that the answers to these questions are vocabulary words that have been taught throughout the unit.

Suggested Remediation: Discuss with children the vocabulary words that were not in the activity. Help children retell definitions in their own words or give examples of the vocabulary words. Ask children to illustrate their favorite vocabulary word from the unit.

WRITING (Recommended Time: 15–20 minutes, uninterrupted)

Teacher Directions: Have children turn to page 22. Make sure they have pencils. Read the prompt aloud and point out the illustration on page 23. Make sure children know to draw their picture on page 24 and write their response on page 25. Then read through the writing checklist on page 27. You may wish to give children scrap paper to use to plan their writing, or permit them to use page 26 as scrap paper.

Tell children:
For the last part of the test, you will draw a picture and write two sentences about a topic I'm about to read to you. The topic explains what you are going to draw and write about. The topic also gives you some ideas for planning.

If you do not know how to spell a word, sound out the word and do the best you can. Write as neatly as you can. Be sure your sentences are about the topic. Here is the topic you should write about:

Prompt:

In "Mittens," Matt takes care of a cat that has kittens. Think of a pet you have or would like to have someday. What type of animal is your pet, or what type of animal would you like for a pet? How do you, or would you, take care of this pet? Tell about your pet and how you take care of it. Draw a picture of you taking care of your pet. Then, write two complete sentences about it.

Point out the picture of Matt and Mittens on page 23. Read the caption: **Matt takes good care of Mittens.** Point out the drawing box on page 24 and the lines on page 25 for writing.

Then point out the checklist on page 27. Read the following to the children:

Here are some things to remember when you are writing and drawing:

Did you draw you and your pet?
Did you think about the pet before writing?

(Writing continued)

Did you tell about how to take care of this pet?
Do your sentences make sense?
Do your sentences begin with a capital letter?
Do your sentences end with a punctuation mark?
Remember to look at your drawing.
Remember to write two complete sentences.
Remember to reread your sentences.

Now, think about what you would like to draw and write. You have twenty minutes. Remember to ask yourself the questions on page 27 after you are finished working. Make sure that you have written two complete sentences.

Be sure to answer any questions children may have. Read the prompt a second time. Alert them when they have 5 minutes remaining.

Scoring: See page vii of this manual for information on how to score Writing.

5-Point Scoring Rubric

5	4	3	2	1
• writing is well focused on the topic	• writing is focused on topic	• writing is mostly focused on topic	• writing is generally focused on topic	• writing is not focused on topic
• idea is very clear	• idea is clear	• idea is mostly clear	• idea is generally clear	• idea is unclear
• sentences are complete	• sentences are mostly complete	• sentences are mostly complete	• sentences are incomplete	• writes only one sentence; incomplete
• voice is engaging; excellent use of writing conventions	• very good use of writing conventions	• good use of writing conventions	• frequent errors in writing conventions	• shows serious errors in writing conventions

Sample Responses:

Possible response (5-point score):

I have a green turtle. I give him food and water.

Possible response (4-point score):

I have a yellow dog. I take him walk.

Possible response (3-point score):

My cat play. It is fun.

Possible response (2-point score):

I want bird. One bird.

Possible response (1-point score):

bunny hop

Unit 1 Test Evaluation Chart

Name ______________________ **Date** ______________

Item	Skill	Week/Day	Item/Type*	Assistance (circle)	Score (circle one)
1	Character and Setting	Week 1 Day 3	MC	Y N	0 1 2
2	Character and Setting	Week 1 Day 3	MC	Y N	0 1 2
3	Compare and Contrast	Week 2 Day 3	MC	Y N	0 1 2
4	Cause and Effect	Week 6 Day 3	MC	Y N	0 1 2
5	Main Idea	Week 4 Day 3	MC	Y N	0 1 2
6	Character and Setting	Week 3 Day 3	MC	Y N	0 1 2
7	Character and Setting	Week 3 Day 3	MC	Y N	0 1 2
8	Compare and Contrast	Week 2 Day 3	MC	Y N	0 1 2
9	Cause and Effect	Week 6 Day 3	MC	Y N	0 1 2
10	Main Idea	Week 4 Day 3	MC	Y N	0 1 2
11	Retelling	Week 5 Day 3	MC	Y N	0 1 2
12	Literary Analysis	Week 1 Day 3	MC	Y N	0 1 2
13	Retelling	Week 4 Day 3	MC	Y N	0 1 2
14	Retelling	Week 5 Day 3	MC	Y N	0 1 2
15	Cause and Effect	Week 6 Day 4	MC	Y N	0 1 2
16	Sentences	Week 1 Day 4	CR	Y N	0 1 2
17	Word Order	Week 4 Day 4	CR	Y N	0 1 2
18	Predicates of Sentences	Week 3 Day 4	CR	Y N	0 1 2
19	Adjectives	Week 3 Day 3	CR	Y N	0 1 2
20	Questions	Week 6 Day 4	CR	Y N	0 1 2
21	/k/ spelled *-ck*	Week 1 Day 2	MC	Y N	0 1 2
22	/ks/ spelled *-x*	Week 2 Day 2	MC	Y N	0 1 2
23	/z/ spelled *-s*	Week 3 Day 2	MC	Y N	0 1 2
24	Sentences	Week 1 Day 4	MC	Y N	0 1 2
25	Sentences	Week 1 Day 4	MC	Y N	0 1 2
26	Short Vowel /a/	Week 1 Day 2	MC	Y N	0 1 2
27	Short Vowel /e/	Week 5 Day 2	MC	Y N	0 1 2
28	Short Vowel /i/	Week 2 Day 2	MC	Y N	0 1 2
29	Short Vowel /o/	Week 3 Day 2	MC	Y N	0 1 2
30	Short Vowel /u/	Week 6 Day 2	MC	Y N	0 1 2
31	Vocabulary	Week 1 Day 1	MC	Y N	0 1 2
32	Vocabulary	Week 1 Day 1	MC	Y N	0 1 2
33	Vocabulary	Week 2 Day 1	MC	Y N	0 1 2
34	Vocabulary	Week 4 Day 1	MC	Y N	0 1 2
35	Vocabulary	Week 3 Day 1	MC	Y N	0 1 2
36	Vocabulary	Week 3 Day 1	CR	Y N	0 1 2
37	Vocabulary	Week 4 Day 1	CR	Y N	0 1 2
38	Vocabulary	Week 5 Day 1	CR	Y N	0 1 2
39	Vocabulary	Week 5 Day 1	CR	Y N	0 1 2
40	Vocabulary	Week 6 Day 1	CR	Y N	0 1 2
SCORE A: Skills and Content					____ **out of 80**
SCORE B: Writing				Y N	4 8 12 16 20
OVERALL SCORE					____ **out of 100**

***MC = multiple choice CR = constructed response**

Grade 1, Unit 2
Answer Key and Directions

COMPREHENSION (Recommended Time: 30–45 minutes, uninterrupted)

<u>**Teacher Directions:**</u> Directions in **bold** are to be read aloud; others are for your information only. Use the following directions to administer the assessment. Make sure all children have a test booklet copy and pencils, and that children are on page 2 of the booklet. Explain that they will listen to a story and then answer some questions about it. Have children look at the picture and follow along as you read. Be sure to pause after each question so that children have time to mark their answers.

Read the following directions:

Now I am going to read a story about a girl named Kate and her bike. After the story, I will ask you some questions. Listen carefully. The story is called "A Bike For Kate." Here is the story.

A Bike for Kate

1 **Kate saw a new bike at the bike shop.**
2 **The bike was green. It had a bell.**
3 **"I like that bike," said Kate.**

Tell children to look over to page 3.

4 **"We cannot get that bike," said Mom.**
5 **But Mom found another bike.**
6 **Mom said, "This bike is old. But I can make it look new."**
7 **"I will wash the bike and paint it green."**

Tell children to turn to page 4.

8 **The bike was very nice now because Mom fixed it up.**
9 **The bike even had a new bell!**
10 **Kate gave Mom a big hug.**

Now model how to fill in the circle. Demonstrate the directions to the children, using a student test book. Read each question twice. Pause after reading a question to give children time to fill in the circle.

Now look at page 5. There are some pictures with circles under them. I will ask you a question about the story. Look at the pictures and fill in the circle under the picture that answers the question. Listen carefully.

1. **Look at the first row of pictures at the top of the page. What did Kate want? Did Kate want *a wagon . . . a unicycle . . .* or *a bike?* Put your finger on the picture that shows what Kate wanted. Then fill in the circle under the picture you chose.**

(Comprehension continued)

2. **Point to the next row of pictures. Who fixed up the bike? Was it *Dad . . . Mom* . . . or *Kate?* Fill in the circle under the picture that shows the best answer.**

3. **Move down to the next row of pictures. What did Mom use to make the bike green? Was it *a box of crayons* . . . *a can of paint* . . . or *a hose?* Fill in the circle under the picture that shows the best answer.**

Turn to page 6.

4. **Look at the top row of pictures. What was the last thing to happen in the story? Was the last thing that happened *Mom painting the bike* . . . *Kate looking at the bike in the store* . . . or *Mom and Kate hugging next to the bike?* Fill in the circle under the picture that shows the best answer.**

5. **Look down at the next row of pictures. Why was the bike very nice now? Was the bike nice now because *Mom painted the bike* . . . *Mom bought a bike* . . . or *Kate rode the bike?* Fill in the circle under the picture that shows the best answer.**

Tell children that you will read another story about Kate, and they will answer questions about the new story. Then read the story with fluency.

Look at page 7. Now I will read you another story about Kate and her mom. Then I will ask you some questions about the story. Here is the story. It's called, "The Bike Path." Listen carefully.

The Bike Path

1 **Kate and Mom rode their bikes to the bike path.**
2 **But the path had huge holes. Litter was on the ground.**
3 **"We need to fix the path," said Mom.**
4 **Mom and Kate asked people to help them.**

Now turn to page 8.

5 **People put cans for trash close to the path.**
6 **People tossed grass seeds on the sides of the path.**
7 **Soon grass was growing.**
8 **Now the path is a good place to ride bikes.**

Remind children that you will now ask them some questions. Read each question twice. Pause after reading a question to give children time to fill in the circle.

Now look at page 9. There are some pictures with circles under them. I will ask you a question about the story. Look at the pictures and listen carefully.

Demonstrate the directions to the children, using a student test book.

6. **Look at the first row of pictures. Where did Mom and Kate go? Did they go to *a bike path* . . . *a classroom* . . . or *a house?* Fill in the circle under the picture that shows the best answer.**

(Comprehension continued)

7. **Put your finger on the next row of pictures. What was on the path? Was it *a car . . . a deer . . .* or *paper and trash?* Fill in the circle under the picture that shows the best answer.**

8. **Move down to the next row of pictures. What was one way people fixed the path? Was it by *mopping the floor . . . picking up trash . . .* or *riding a bike?* Fill in the circle under the picture that shows the best answer.**

Now turn to page 10.

9. **Look at the first row of pictures. Who fixed up the path? Was it *adults and children . . . a boy . . .* or *a girl?* Fill in the circle under the picture that shows the best answer.**

10. **Put your finger on the next row of pictures. Why is the path a good place to ride now? Is it because the path *is clean . . . has animals on it . . .* or *has a stop sign?* Fill in the circle under the picture that shows the best answer.**

Scoring: Photocopy and use the evaluation chart to track student scores and progress.

Comprehension Answer Key with Interpretation:

1. What did Kate want?

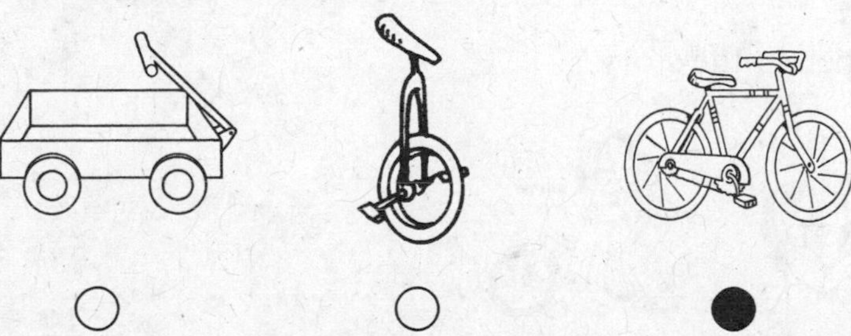

Children who chose the first picture (a wagon) may not distinguish between bikes and other wheeled toys.

Children who chose the second picture (a unicycle) may not distinguish between bikes and other wheeled toys.

Correct answer: third picture (a bike)

2. Who fixed up the bike?

(Comprehension continued)

Children who chose the first picture (Dad) may have chosen the first figure shown.

Correct answer: second picture (Mom)

Children who chose the third picture (Kate) may have thought the question was asking for whom the bike was being fixed.

3. What did Mom use to make the bike green?

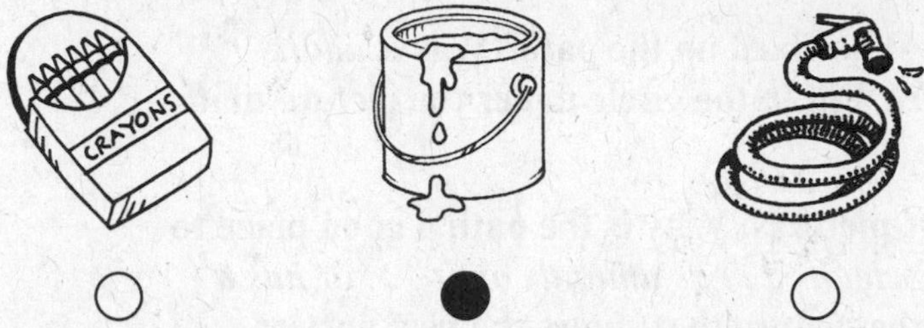

Children may have chosen the first picture (a box of crayons) because crayons can be used to color things.

Correct answer: second picture (a can of paint)

Children may have chosen the third picture (a hose) because the bike was washed as well as painted.

4. What was the *last* thing to happen in the story?

Children may have chosen the first picture (Mom painting bike) because it shows Mom's solution.

Children may have chosen the second picture (girl pointing at bike in store window) because it shows Kate wanting the bike.

Correct answer: third picture (Mom and girl hugging next to newly painted bike)

5. Why was the bike very nice now?

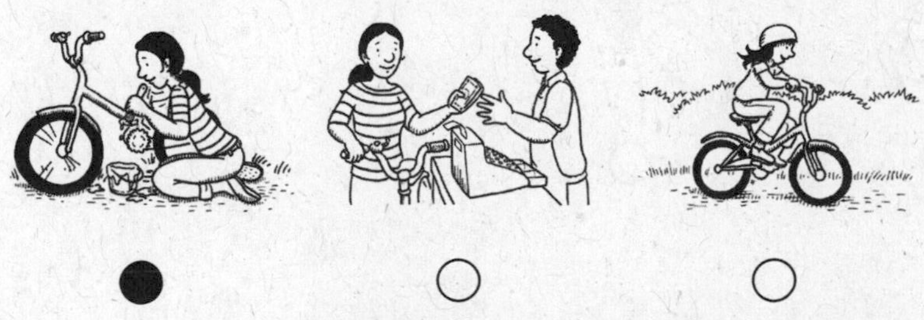

(Comprehension continued)

Correct answer: first picture (Mom painting bike)

Children may have chosen the second picture (Mom buying bike at store) because a new bike would look nice.

Children may have chosen the third picture (girl riding bike) because it shows the bike being used.

6. Where did Mom and Kate go?

Correct answer: first picture (a bike path)

Children may have chosen the second picture (a classroom) because it is a place where many children go.

Children may have chosen the third picture (a house) because Kate and Mom would begin their ride at home.

7. What was on the path?

Children may have chosen the first picture (a car) because bikes and cars often share roads.

Children may have chosen the second picture (a deer) because an animal might be seen on a path.

Correct answer: third picture (paper and trash by bike path)

8. What was one way people fixed the path?

(Comprehension continued)

Children may have chosen the first picture (a person mopping the floor) because mopping is a way to clean.

Correct answer: second picture (two people picking up trash)

Children may have chosen the third picture (a woman riding a bike) because the story features a bike path.

9. Who fixed up the path?

Correct answer: first picture (adults and children)

Children may have chosen a boy because they did not distinguish between a group of people and an individual.

Children may have chosen a girl because they did not distinguish between a group of people and an individual.

10. Why is the path a good place to ride now?

Correct answer: first picture (a clean path)

Children may have chosen the second picture (a deer) because you might see a deer on a path.

Children may have chosen the third picture (a stop sign) because stop signs make roads safe.

<u>**Suggested Remediation:**</u> Discuss each story, using the pictures and words to identify the main ideas and details. Help children retell the stories in their own words.

CHECKING SKILLS (Recommended Time: 20 minutes, uninterrupted)

Teacher Directions: Use the following directions to administer the assessment. Tell children that in this part of the test they will answer questions about the words in sentences. Review how to complete a multiple-choice item by filling in a circle. Read each sentence and question twice. Be sure to pause after each question so that children have time to mark their answers. Make sure all children are on page 11 before you begin.

Tell children:

I will read a sentence from one of the stories and ask a question about it. Then I will read the answer choices. Fill in the circle under the word that answers the question.

11. Kate gave Mom a big hug. Which word is a noun? Is it *gave* . . . *big* . . . or *hug?* Fill in the circle under the best answer.

12. Kate saw a new bike at the bike shop. Which word is a proper noun? Is it *shop* . . . *bike* . . . or *Kate?* Fill in the circle underthe best answer.

13. Now the path is a good place to ride bikes. Which word is a plural noun? Is it *bikes* . . . *path* . . . or *place?* Fill in the circle under the best answer.

Turn to page 12.

14. The green bike had a bell. How many nouns are in the sentence? Is it *one* . . *two* . . . or *three?* Fill in the circle next to the best answer.

15. People tossed grass seeds on the sides of the path. Which word is a singular noun that names one thing? Is it *seeds* . . . *sides* . . . or *path?* Fill in the circle next to the best answer.

Look at page 13. Follow along as I read each sentence. Then I will ask you a question. Write your answer on the line.

16. Litter was on the ground.
What are the nouns in the sentence?

17. The bike was for Kate.
What is the proper noun in the sentence?

18. The bike was very nice now because Mom painted it.
What word helps us tell why something happened?

Turn to page 14. I will read a sentence. Then I will ask you a question. In your book, circle the word or words that tell the answer.

19. Soon grass was growing.
What words tell what happened?

(Checking Skills continued)

20. kate, rick, and matt picked up litter.
What nouns should begin with capital letters?

<u>**Scoring:**</u> Photocopy and use the evaluation chart to track student scores and progress.

<u>**Checking Skills Answer Key with Interpretation:**</u>

11. Kate gave Mom a big hug. Which word is a noun?

    Correct answer: *hug*

    Children who responded *gave* or *big* may not understand that a noun is a naming word.

12. Kate saw a new bike at the bike shop. Which word is a proper noun?

    Correct answer: *Kate*

    Children who responded *shop* or *bike* may not understand that a proper noun names a specific person, place, or thing.

13. Now the path is a good place to ride bikes. Which word is a plural noun?

    Correct answer: *bikes*

    Children who responded *path* or *place* may not understand that plural nouns are nouns that name more than one thing and often end in *-s.*

14. The green bike had a bell. How many nouns are in the sentence?

    Correct answer: *two*

    Children who responded *one* or *three* may have miscounted the nouns in the sentence.

15. People tossed grass seeds on the sides of the path. Which word is a singular noun that names one thing?

    Correct answer: *path*

    Children who responded *seeds* or *sides* may not understand that a singular noun names one thing.

16. Litter was on the ground. What are the nouns in the sentence?

    Correct answer: *litter, ground*

    Children who chose *was, on,* or *the* may not distinguish nouns from other parts of speech.

17. The bike was for Kate. What is the proper noun in the sentence?

    Correct answer: *Kate*

    Children who answered otherwise may not distinguish common and proper nouns.

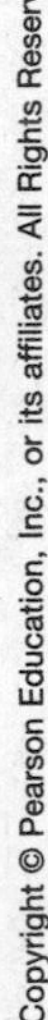

(Checking Skills continued)

18. The bike was very nice now because Mom painted it. What word helps us tell why something happened?

    Correct answer: *because*

    Children who answered otherwise may have chosen the cause or effect rather than the signal word.

19. Soon grass was growing. What words tell what happened?

    Correct answer: *was growing*

    Children who answered otherwise may not distinguish verbs, or action words, from other parts of speech.

20. kate, rick, and matt picked up litter. What nouns should begin with capital letters?

    Correct answer: *Kate, Rick, Matt*

    Children who answered otherwise may not have circled all three proper nouns or may have circled the common noun as well as the proper nouns.

<u>**Suggested Remediation:**</u> Work with children to review nouns. Define nouns, verbs, and adjectives, giving examples of each. Have children name objects in the classroom. Help them distinguish proper names of people and common nouns that name people. Use classroom objects to develop the concept of one and more than one to teach singular and plural noun forms.

WORD ANALYSIS (Recommended Time: 20–30 minutes, uninterrupted)

<u>**Teacher Directions:**</u> Have children turn to page 15. Explain to them that in this part of the test, you will say a word. Instruct them to fill in the circle under the word. Point out the picture that illustrates the word.

Tell children:

I am going to read a word. Look at the words written in your book. Choose the word that you heard. You may say the word aloud before you decide. Fill in the circle under the word.

21. **Put your finger on the picture at the top of the page. What do you see in the picture? Next look at the three words. Does the picture show *a sip . . . a ship . . .* or *a shop?* Fill in the circle under the word you chose.**

22. **Look at the second picture. Does the picture show *a cube . . . curl . . .* or *a cub?* Fill in the circle under the word you chose.**

23. **Point to the third picture. Does that picture show *a rack . . . a lake . . .* or *a rake?* Fill in the circle under the word you chose.**

Have children turn to page 16. Tell children that in this part of the test, they will match each picture to its name. Instruct them to fill in the circle in front of the word that names the picture.

(Word Analysis continued)

Look at the picture in your book. Look at the words next to the picture. Choose the word that tells what the picture shows. You may say each word aloud before you decide. Fill in the circle next to the word.

24. Does the picture show *a bun . . . a bone . . .* or *dome?* Fill in the circle next to the word you choose.

25. Does the picture show *a sheet . . . a shape . . .* or *a sheep?* Fill in the circle next to the word you choose.

Have children move to page 17. Tell children that in this part of the test, they will circle words in sentences that have the same vowel sound as a picture name. Point out that they may have to circle more than one word in a sentence. Read each sentence twice. Model how to circle answers in a sentence.

Look at the pictures in your book. I will read a word that tells what the picture shows. Then I will read a sentence. Circle the words in the sentence that have the same long vowel sound as the word from the picture.

26. This picture shows a gate. The sentence is *Jan will take me to the game.* Which two words in the sentence have the same vowel sound as *gate?* Circle those two words.

27. This picture shows a dime. The sentence is *Do you like to hike and swim?* Which two words in the sentence have the same vowel sound as *dime?* Circle those two words.

28. This picture shows a rope. The sentence is *Jason sent a note to his brother at home.* Which two words in the sentence have the same vowel sound as *rope?* Circle those two words.

Turn to page 18.

Tell children that in this part of the test, they will write letters to complete the name of a picture and then they will write the whole word. Demonstrate how to complete the activity.

Look at the picture in your book. Say the word. Write the letters that make the beginning sound. Then write the whole word.

29. What do you see in the picture? The last letters are *eese.* Fill in the missing letters. Then write the whole word on the next line.

30. What do you see in the picture? The last letters are *ale.* Fill in the missing letters. Then write the whole word on the next line.

Scoring: Photocopy and use the evaluation chart to track children's scores and progress.

Word Analysis Answer Key with Interpretation:

21. **Correct answer:** *ship*

(Word Analysis continued)

Children who answered *sip* may not distinguish /s/ from /sh/.

Children who answered *shop* may not have listened carefully to the medial sound.

22. **Correct answer:** *cube*

Children who answered *curl* may not distinguish the ending sound.

Children who answered *cub* may not distinguish long and short *u* sounds.

23. **Correct answer:** *rake*

Children who answered *rack* may not recognize the *a _ e* pattern of long *a*.

Children who answered *lake* may not distinguish the beginning sound.

24. **Correct answer:** *bone*

Children who answered *bun* may not distinguish the short *u* and long *o* sounds.

Children who answered *dome* may confuse the letters *b* and *d*.

25. **Correct answer:** *sheep*

Children who answered *sheet* may not distinguish the ending sound.

Children who answered *shape* may have chosen the word with the correct beginning and end sounds.

26. **Correct answer:** *take, game*

Children who gave incorrect answers may have circled all words that have the letter *a* rather than associating vowel sounds and patterns.

27. **Correct answer:** *like, hike*

Children who gave incorrect answers may have circled all words that have the letter *i* rather than associating vowel sounds and patterns.

28. **Correct answer:** *note, home*

Children who gave incorrect answers may have circled all words that have the letter *o* rather than associating vowel sounds and patterns.

29. **Correct response:** *c h eese cheese*

Children who gave incorrect letters may have written *c* rather than *ch* to complete the word.

30. **Correct response:** *w h ale whale*

Children who gave incorrect letters may have written *w* rather than *wh* to complete the word.

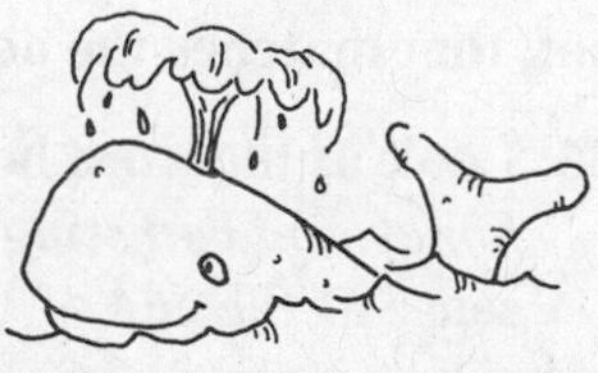

Suggested Remediation: Review the long vowel patterns *vowel + e,* vowel digraph *ee,* and consonant digraphs *sh* and *th.* Say pairs of words with and without the pattern you are reviewing and have children clap when they hear the word with the review pattern. For example, have children clap when they hear the long *a* sound in these pairs: *cap, cape; tame, tam; tack, take.* Write the long vowel words on the board and underline the vowel pattern. Give children pictures and have them sort them by vowel sounds or by the consonant digraphs *ch* and *wh.*

VOCABULARY (Recommended Time: 20–30 minutes, uninterrupted)

Teacher Directions: Have children turn to page 19. Tell children that they will work with vocabulary in this part of the test. Then tell children that in the first part of this test, you will read a sentence. Children are to choose a picture that goes with the sentence. Show children how to fill in the circle for the answer.

Read the following directions to children:
I will say a sentence that talks about one of the pictures you see in your book. Fill in the circle under the correct picture.

31. Here is the sentence: *These insects have wings and six legs.* Now, which picture matches this sentence best? *These insects have wings and six legs.* Fill in the circle under the picture you choose.

32. Here is the next sentence: *The box is under the bed.* Now, which picture matches this sentence best? *The box is under the bed.* Fill in the circle under the picture you choose.

33. Here is the next sentence: *The family sat down to eat a meal.* Now, which picture matches this sentence best? *The family sat down to eat a meal.* Fill in the circle under the picture you choose.

Turn to page 20.

34. Here is the next sentence: *Litter is on the ground.* Now, which picture matches this sentence best? *Litter is on the ground.* Fill in the circle under the picture you choose.

35. Here is the last sentence: *Ben can wash the dish.* Now, which picture matches this sentence best? *Ben can wash the dish.* Fill in the circle under the picture you choose.

Have children look at page 21. Tell them that you will read a list of words and then you will read a definition of one word. Children are to choose the word with that meaning from the list and write the word. Read each definition twice.

I will say a definition of a word you have learned. Choose the word from the box that matches the definition. Write the word in your book.

36. Look at the word box. Here is the definition: F*lying insects that make honey and can sting you are* ________. Write the word that makes the most sense at the end of this sentence.

(Vocabulary continued)

37. **Here is the second definition:** ***An empty space or opening in something is a ________.*** **Write the word that makes the most sense at the end of this sentence.**

38. **Here is the third definition:** ***Someone who is trained to help doctors and take care of people who are sick and injured is a ________.*** **Write the word that makes the most sense at the end of this sentence.**

39. **Here is the next definition:** ***To come together in a group is to ________.*** **Write the word that makes the most sense at the end of this sentence.**

40. **Here is the final definition:** ***To come back or to go back to a place is to ________.*** **Write the word that makes the most sense at the end of this sentence.**

<u>Scoring</u>: Photocopy and use the evaluation chart to track student scores and progress.

<u>Vocabulary Answer Key with Interpretation:</u>

31. These **insects** have wings and six legs.

Children who chose the first picture (flying birds) may have focused on wings rather than the word *insect.*

Correct response: second picture (flying bees)

Children who chose the third picture (ants) may have focused only on the number of legs an insect has.

32. The box is **under** the bed.

Correct answer: first picture (gift box under a bed)

Children who chose the second picture (gift box on a bed) may not understand location words.

Children who chose the third picture (gift box on a shelf) may not understand location words.

(Vocabulary continued)

33. The **family** sat down to eat a **meal.**

Children who chose the first picture (one person eating) may not have considered the meaning of *family.*

Children who chose the second picture (a family at a park) may not have focused on the family activity.

Correct answer: third picture (a family eating dinner at a table)

34. **Litter** is on the **ground.**

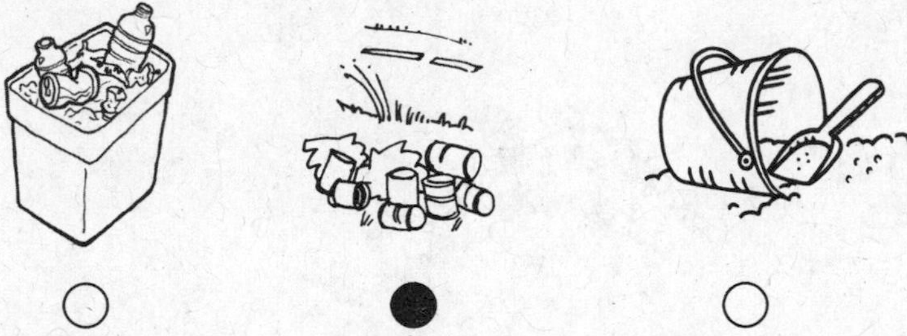

Children who chose the first picture (trash in a trashcan) may not have focused on the location of the litter.

Correct answer: second picture (litter on the ground)

Children who chose the third picture (a bucket of sand) may not understand the meaning of *litter.*

35. Ben can **wash** the dish.

Children who chose the first picture (a boy washing a dog) may not have focused on the object of the sentence.

Children who chose the second picture (a woman washing a car) may have focused only on the verb in the sentence.

Correct answer: third picture (a boy washing dishes)

(Vocabulary continued)

36. **Correct response:** *bees*

    Children who answered incorrectly may not understand the definition of *bees.*

37. **Correct response:** *hole*

    Children who answered incorrectly may not understand the definition of *hole.*

38. **Correct response:** *nurse*

    Children who answered incorrectly may not understand the definition of *nurse.*

39. **Correct response:** *gather*

    Children who answered incorrectly may not understand the definition of *gather.*

40. **Correct response:** *return*

    Children who answered incorrectly may not understand the definition of *return.*

Suggested Remediation: Review the constructed-response sentences. Discuss all the information provided in the sentences. Then help children identify the answer that best fits the information. Review the unit's vocabulary with children. Use word and definition cards. Have children draw pictures on the word cards to help with identification. Then have children match the word cards with their definition cards.

WRITING (Recommended Time: 15–20 minutes, uninterrupted)

Teacher Directions: Have children turn to page 22. Make sure they have pencils. Read the prompt aloud and point out the illustration on page 23. Make sure children know to draw their picture on page 24 and write their response on page 25. Then read through the writing checklist on page 27. You may wish to give children scrap paper to use to plan their writing, or permit them to use page 26 as scrap paper.

Tell children:

For the last part of the test, you will draw a picture and write at least two sentences about a topic I'm about to read to you. The topic explains what you are going to draw and write about. The topic also gives you some ideas for planning.

If you do not know how to spell a word, sound out the word and do the best you can. Write as neatly as you can. Be sure your sentences are about the topic. Here is the topic you should draw and write about:

(Writing continued)

Prompt:

Mom helps Kate in "A Bike for Kate" by fixing up a bike for Kate. Think about your family. How do people in your family help you? How do you help people in your family? Draw a picture that shows these things. Then, write at least two complete sentences about it.

Point out the picture of Mom painting the bike on page 23. Read the caption: **Here is Kate's Mom making the old bike look new.** Point out the drawing box on page 24 and the lines on page 25 for writing.

Point out the checklist on page 27. Read the following to children:

Here are some things to remember when you are drawing and writing:
Did you draw your family members helping?
Did you think about how family members help each other before writing?
Did you tell what you or you family members do to help?
Do your sentences make sense?
Do your sentences begin with a capital letter?
Do your sentences end with a punctuation mark?
Remember to look at your drawing.
Remember to write at least two complete sentences.
Remember to reread your sentences.

Now, think about what you would like to draw and write. You have twenty minutes. Remember to ask yourself the questions on page 27 after you are finished working. Make sure you write at least two complete sentences.

Be sure to answer any questions children may have. Read the prompt a second time. Alert them when they have five minutes remaining.

Scoring: See page xi of this manual for information on how to score Writing.

5-Point Scoring Rubric

5	4	3	2	1
• writing is well focused on topic	• writing focuses on topic	• writing mostly focuses on topic	• writing does not remain on topic	• writing is not focused
• contains clear ideas	• most ideas are clear	• some ideas are clear	• many ideas are not clear	• ideas are unclear
• excellent use of correct grammar	• good use of correct grammar	• fairly good use of correct grammar	• grammar rules are sometimes not followed	• grammar rules are not followed
• sentences are complete	• most sentences are complete	• many sentences are complete	• many sentences are incomplete	• incomplete sentences
• uses correct capitalization	• uses correct capitalization most of the time	• capitalization rules mostly followed	• some words are not properly capitalized	• little or no attention to capitalization rules
• sentences are punctuated correctly	• most sentences are punctuated correctly	• many sentences are punctuated correctly	• few sentences are punctuated correctly	• sentences are not punctuated

(Writing continued)

Sample Responses:

Possible response (5-point score):

My family makes meals together. Mom and Dad cook. I put the food on the table.

Possible response (4-point score):

I help with pet. We feed dog. I put water in dish.

Possible response (3-point score):

Grandma visit. Dad has two bag. She hug.

Possible response (2-point score):

Dad read Dog barks. hold bear.

Possible response (1-point score):

we are work.

FLUENCY (Time: 5–10 minutes preparation; 1 minute per child for reading)

Teacher Directions: Please refer to the "General Directions for Oral Reading Fluency Assessment" in this Teacher's Manual. Make enough copies of the following pages for each child. Do not provide children with a copy until test time.

Say these specific directions to the child:

When I say "Begin," start reading aloud at the top of this page. Read across the page (DEMONSTRATE BY POINTING). **Try to read each word. If you come to a word you don't know, I will say the word for you. Read as quickly and accurately as you can, but do not read so fast that you make mistakes. Do your best reading.**

Name ______________________________ Date ______________

Unit 2 Fluency **Teacher Copy**

Say these specific directions to the student:
When I say "Begin," start reading aloud at the top of this page. Read across the page (DEMONSTRATE BY POINTING). *Try to read each word. If you come to a word you don't know, I will say the word for you. Read as quickly and accurately as you can, but do not read SO fast that you make mistakes. Do your best reading.*

A Hike to the Lake

Nate and Dad take the bus to the woods. 9
Nate and Dad hike on the path. 16
Nate runs. "Do not rush," said Dad. 23
"We have lots of time." 28

Nate and Dad hike to a little lake. 36
Nate and Dad put their feet in the water. 45
The water is not too hot. 51

Nate sees a big duck and three little ducks. 60
The little ducks quack and quack. 66
"Look, Dad," said Nate. "See the fish." 73
Dad smiles. Dad sees nine fish. 79

Nate and Dad hike back to the bus. 87
They ride the bus home. 92
Nate and Dad had a good time. 99

EVALUATING CODES FOR ORAL READING

sky (crossed out)	(/)	word read incorrectly
blue ^ sky	(^)	inserted word
	(])	after the last word read

Comments:

FLUENCY SCORE

Number of Words Read per Minute: ________

Number of Errors ________

Number of Words Read Correctly: ________

Errors include the following: 1) words read incorrectly; 2) words left out or inserted; 3) mispronounced words; 4) dropped endings or sounds; and 5) reversals. Self corrections and word repetitions are NOT marked as errors.

Name ______________________________ Date ______________

Unit 2 Fluency **Student Copy**

A Hike to the Lake

Nate and Dad take the bus to the woods.
Nate and Dad hike on the path.
Nate runs. "Do not rush," said Dad.
"We have lots of time."

Nate and Dad hike to a little lake.
Nate and Dad put their feet in the water.
The water is not too hot.

Nate sees a big duck and three little ducks.
The little ducks quack and quack.
"Look, Dad," said Nate. "See the fish."
Dad smiles. Dad sees nine fish.

Nate and Dad hike back to the bus.
They ride the bus home.
Nate and Dad had a good time.

Unit 2 Test Evaluation Chart

Name ______________________________ **Date** ______________

Item	Skill	Week/Day	Item/Type*	Assistance (circle)	Score (circle one)
1	Main Idea and Details	Week 1 Day 3	MC	Y N	0 1 2
2	Main Idea and Details	Week 1 Day 3	MC	Y N	0 1 2
3	Main Idea and Details	Week 2 Day 3	MC	Y N	0 1 2
4	Sequence	Week 4 Day 3	MC	Y N	0 1 2
5	Cause and Effect	Week 2 Day 3	MC	Y N	0 1 2
6	Main Idea and Details	Week 1 Day 3	MC	Y N	0 1 2
7	Main Idea and Details	Week 1 Day 3	MC	Y N	0 1 2
8	Main Idea and Details	Week 1 Day 3	MC	Y N	0 1 2
9	Main Idea and Details	Week 1 Day 3	MC	Y N	0 1 2
10	Cause and Effect	Week 2 Day 3	MC	Y N	0 1 2
11	Nouns	Week 1 Day 4	MC	Y N	0 1 2
12	Proper Nouns	Week 2 Day 4	MC	Y N	0 1 2
13	Plural Nouns	Week 5 Day 4	MC	Y N	0 1 2
14	Nouns	Week 1 Day 4	MC	Y N	0 1 2
15	Singular Nouns	Week 5 Day 4	MC	Y N	0 1 2
16	Nouns	Week 1 Day 4	CR	Y N	0 1 2
17	Proper Nouns	Week 2 Day 4	CR	Y N	0 1 2
18	Cause and Effect	Week 2 Day 2	CR	Y N	0 1 2
19	Verbs	Week 1 Day 3	CR	Y N	0 1 2
20	Proper Nouns	Week 2 Day 4	CR	Y N	0 1 2
21	/sh/ Spelled sh	Week 1 Day 2	MC	Y N	0 1 2
22	Long *u* Spelled *u_e*	Week 5 Day 2	MC	Y N	0 1 2
23	Long *a* Spelled *a_e*	Week 2 Day 2	MC	Y N	0 1 2
24	Long *o* Spelled *o_e*	Week 4 Day 2	MC	Y N	0 1 2
25	Long *e* Spelled *ee*	Week 6 Day 2	MC	Y N	0 1 2
26	Long *a* Spelled *a_e*	Week 2 Day 2	CR	Y N	0 1 2
27	Long *i* Spelled *i_e*	Week 3 Day 2	CR	Y N	0 1 2
28	Long *o* Spelled *o_e*	Week 4 Day 2	CR	Y N	0 1 2
29	/ch/ Spelled *ch*	Week 3 Day 2	CR	Y N	0 1 2
30	/wh/ Spelled *wh*	Week 3 Day 2	CR	Y N	0 1 2
31	Vocabulary	Week 6 Day 1	MC	Y N	0 1 2
32	Vocabulary	Week 4 Day 1	MC	Y N	0 1 2
33	Vocabulary	Week 1 Day 1	MC	Y N	0 1 2
34	Vocabulary	Week 3 Day 1	MC	Y N	0 1 2
35	Vocabulary	Week 1 Day 1	MC	Y N	0 1 2
36	Vocabulary	Week 1 Day 1	CR	Y N	0 1 2
37	Vocabulary	Week 4 Day 1	CR	Y N	0 1 2
38	Vocabulary	Week 2 Day 1	CR	Y N	0 1 2
39	Vocabulary	Week 1 Day 1	CR	Y N	0 1 2
40	Vocabulary	Week 6 Day 1	CR	Y N	0 1 2
SCORE A: Skills and Content					____ **out of 80**
SCORE B: Writing Sentences					2 4 6 8 10
SCORE C: Fluency				**WCPM** ____	2 4 6 8 10
OVERALL SCORE					____ **out of 100**

***MC = multiple choice CR = constructed response**

Grade 1, Unit 3
Answer Key and Directions

COMPREHENSION (Recommended Time: 30–45 minutes, uninterrupted)

Teacher Directions: Directions in **bold** are to be read aloud; others are for your information only. Use the following directions to administer the assessment. Make sure all children have a test booklet copy and pencils, and that children are on page 2 of the booklet.

Explain that they will listen to a story and then answer some questions about it. Have students look at the picture and follow along as you read. Be sure to pause after each question so that children have time to mark their answers.

Read the following to the children:

Now I am going to read a story about some friends who want to have a picnic outside. After the story, I will ask you some questions. Listen carefully. The story is called "Rainy Day Picnic." Here is the story.

Rainy Day Picnic

1 **Lin and two friends were playing in the park.**

2 **The girls had food in their bags.**

3 **The girls planned to eat outside.**

4 **"The sky is cloudy," Lin said. "Do you think it will rain?"**

Tell children to look on the next page.

5 **Soon the girls could feel big drops of water.**

6 **It was raining!**

7 **The girls picked up their bags. They ran with Lin's Mom into the building.**

8 **"What can we do?" said Lin.**

Tell children to turn to page 4.

9 **"We can't eat outside," said Lin's mom. "But we can eat inside."**

10 **First, the girls put a cloth down.**

11 **Then they sat down.**

12 **Next, the girls ate their food.**

13 **The girls had fun eating inside.**

Now model how to fill in the circle. Demonstrate the directions to the students using a student test book. Read each question twice.

(Comprehension continued)

Tell the children:

Now look at page 5. I am going to ask you some questions about the story. For each question that I ask, you will see three pictures in a row. Ask yourself which picture goes with the question I ask. Fill in the circle below the picture that shows the best answer. Listen carefully.

1. **Look at the first row of pictures at the top of the page. Where were the girls? Were they in *a classroom . . . a park . . .* or *a house?* Put your finger on the picture that shows where the girls were. Then fill in the circle below the picture you chose.**
2. **Point to the next row of pictures. What happened while the girls were playing? Did it start to *rain . . . snow . . .* or *was it sunny?* Fill in the circle below the picture that shows the best answer.**

Now turn to page 6. I am going to ask you some more questions about the story. For each question that I ask, I will read three sentences. Read along with me. Ask yourself which sentence best answers the question. Fill in the circle next to the sentence that is the best answer. Listen carefully.

3. **What problem did the rain cause? Was it *The sky was cloudy . . . The girls got wet . . .* or *The girls could not eat outside?* Fill in the circle next to the sentence that best answers the question *What problem did the rain cause?***
4. **How did the girls solve the problem? Was it *The girls ate inside . . . The girls rode their bikes home . . .* or *The girls waited for the sun to shine?* Fill in the circle next to the sentence that best answers the question *How did the girls solve the problem?***
5. **What was the first thing the girls did in the building? Was it *The girls sat down . . . The girls ate their food . . .* or *The girls put a cloth down?* Fill in the circle next to the sentence that best answers the question *What was the first thing the girls did in the building?***

Look at page 7. Now I am going to read some instructions. These instructions tell you how to make ice pops. Then I will ask you some questions. Listen carefully. Here is "Making Ice Pops."

Making Ice Pops

1 **You can make ice pops.**
2 **Here is what you do.**
3 **First, get five small paper cups.**
4 **Then put fruit juice in the cups.**
5 **Put the cups inside the freezer.**
6 **Wait one hour.**
7 **Then put sticks inside the cups.**

(Comprehension continued)

Now turn to page 8.

8 **Freeze the cups for one day.**
9 **Take a cup out of the freezer.**
10 **Then peel the paper cup off the ice pop.**
11 **Last, eat your ice pop.**

Now you know how to make ice pops. Look at page 9, and I will ask you some questions about making ice pops. Fill in the circle below the picture that best answers the questions.

6. **Look at the first row of pictures. What do you get first to make ice pops? Is it *milk* . . . *an ice tray* . . . or *paper cups?* Put your finger on the picture that shows what you need to get first to make ice pops. Then fill in the circle below that picture.**

7. **Move down to the next row of pictures. How many cups do you need? Is it *three* . . . *five* . . . or *nine?* Fill in the circle below the picture that tells how many cups you need.**

8. **Point to the next row of pictures. What is the *last* thing you put in the cups? Is it *sticks* . . . *juice* . . . or *ice?* Fill in the circle below the picture you choose.**

Ask children to turn to page 10.

Now I am going to ask you some questions. Then I will read three sentences. Read along with me. Fill in the circle next to the sentence that best answers the question I ask.

9. **What do you do *before* putting the cups in the freezer? Is it *Put sticks in the cups* . . . *Pour fruit juice in the cups* . . . or *Take a drink?* Fill in the circle next to the sentence that you choose.**

10. **What is the *last* thing you do *before* eating the ice pops? Is it *Peel off the paper cups* . . . *Eat the ice pops* . . . or *Fill the cups?* Fill in the circle next to the sentence that you choose.**

<u>**Scoring:**</u> Photocopy and use the evaluation chart to track children's scores and progress.

<u>**Comprehension Answer Key with Interpretation:**</u>

1. Where were the girls?

Children may have thought the girls ran into a school building in the first picture.

Correct answer: second picture (park)

Children may not distinguish between a house and other kinds of buildings in the third picture.

(Comprehension continued)

2. What happened while the girls were playing?

● ○ ○

Correct response: first picture (rain)

Children may have chosen this picture (snow) because it shows precipitation.

Children may have chosen this picture (sun) because they confused what the girls had wanted to happen with what actually had happened.

3. What problem did the rain cause?

○ The sky was cloudy.

Children may know that the skies are cloudy when it rains.

○ The girls got wet.

Children may have assumed the girls got wet when it began to rain.

● The girls could not eat outside.

Correct answer

4. How did the girls solve the problem?

● The girls ate inside.

Correct answer

○ The girls rode their bikes home.

Children may have thought the girls would want to go home.

○ The girls waited for the sun to shine.

Children may have thought the girls would wait for the rain to stop.

5. What was the first thing the girls did in the building?

○ The girls sat down.

Children may not have focused on the word *first*.

○ The girls ate their food.

Children may not have focused on the word *first*.

(Comprehension continued)

● The girls put a cloth down.

Correct answer

6. What do you get first to make ice pops?

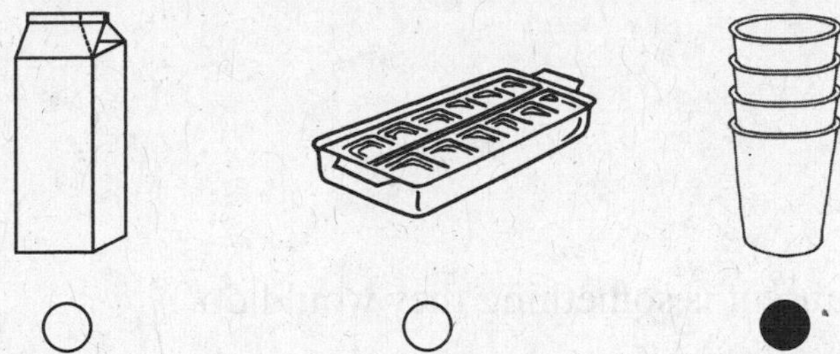

○ ○ ●

Children may have chosen this because the steps call for a liquid.

Children may have chosen this because the activity tells how to make an ice treat.

Correct answer: third picture (paper cups)

7. How many cups do you need?

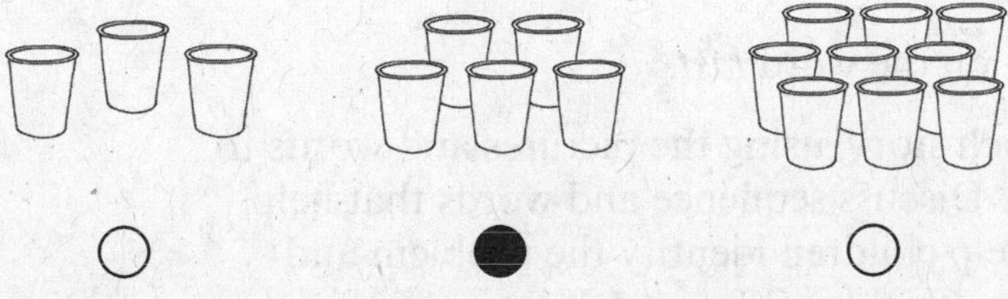

○ ● ○

Children may not have listened carefully to details.

Correct answer: second picture (five paper cups)

Children may not have listened carefully to details.

8. What is the *last* thing you put in the cups?

● ○ ○

Correct answer: first picture (sticks)

Children may not have focused on the word *last*.

Children may have chosen this because the activity describes making an ice treat.

(Comprehension continued)

9. What do you do *before* putting the cups in the freezer?

○ Put sticks in the cups.

Children may not have focused on the word *before*.

● Pour fruit juice in the cups.

Correct answer

○ Take a drink.

Children may have chosen this because it is something they would do.

10. What is the *last* thing you do *before* eating the ice pops?

● Peel off the paper cups.

Correct answer

○ Eat the ice pops.

Children may not have focused on the word *before*.

○ Fill the cups.

Children may not have focused on the word *last*.

Suggested Remediation: Discuss each story, using the pictures and words to identify the main ideas and details. Discuss sequence and words that help us identify when things happen. Help children identify the problem and solution in the first reading selection. Help children retell the stories in their own words.

CHECKING SKILLS (Recommended Time: 20 minutes, uninterrupted)

<u>Teacher Directions:</u> Use the following directions to administer the assessment. Read the sentences aloud more than once if needed. Be sure to pause after each question so that children have time to mark their answers. Make sure all children are on page 11 before you begin.

Read the following to the children:

Now I am going to read some sentences to you. The sentences I will read tell about the story "Rainy Day Picnic." Read the sentences along with me. I will ask you a question about each sentence. You need to pick the word that answers each question. Listen carefully.

11. Which word helps tell things in order in the following sentence? *First, the girls put a cloth down.* Is it *First . . . put . . .* or *down?* Fill in the circle near the word that tells order in the sentence *First, the girls put a cloth down.*

12. Which word is a verb in the following sentence? *Then they sat down.* Is it *They . . . sat . . .* or *. . . down?* Fill in the circle near the word that is a verb in the sentence *Then they sat down.*

13. Which word is an action verb in the following sentence? *Next, the girls ate their food.* Is it *girls . . . ate . . .* or *food?* Fill in the circle near the word that is an action verb in the sentence *Next, the girls ate their food.*

Now turn to page 12.

14. Which word is a contraction in the following sentence? *"We can't eat outside," said Lin's mom.* Is it *can't . . . outside . . .* or *said?* Fill in the circle near the word that is a contraction in the sentence *"We can't eat outside," said Lin's mom.*

15. Which word is a verb that tells about the past in the following sentence? *The girls picked up their bags.* Is it *girls . . . picked . . .* or *their?* Fill in the circle near the word that is a verb that tells about the past. The sentence is *The girls picked up their bags.*

Look at page 13. I will read two verbs and a sentence. Choose the past tense of the verb to finish the sentence. Then write the verb on the line.

16. The girls ________ their bags. Which is the past tense verb to finish the sentence? Is it *packs,* or is it *packed?* Write the word on the line.

17. Lin ________ into the building. Which is the past tense verb to finish the sentence? Is it *walk,* or is it *walked?* Write the word on the line.

18. The girls ________ tag. Which is the past tense verb to finish the sentence? Is it *played,* or is it *playing?* Write the word on the line.

Turn to page 14. I will read you two pairs of sentences. Choose the correct word from the box to finish each sentence. Write the word on the line.

19. Dogs are ________. Are dogs *first . . . now . . .* or *pets?* Write the word you chose on the line. Cats are ________. Are cats *first . . . now . . .* or *pets?* Write the word you chose on the line.

20. At ________, I was small. Which word completes this sentence: *first . . . now . . .* or *pets*? Write the word you chose on the line. ________, I am big. Which word completes the sentence: *first . . . now . . .* or *pets*? Write the word you chose on the line.

(Checking Skills continued)

Scoring: Photocopy and use the evaluation chart to track student scores and progress.

Key: Checking Skills Answer Key with Interpretation

11. First, the girls put a cloth down.

● First

Correct response

○ put

Children may choose the action word rather than the order word.

○ down

Children may confuse the adverb that tells where with the one that tells when.

12. Then they sat down.

○ They

Children may not distinguish between nouns and verbs.

● sat

Correct response

○ down

Children may confuse the adverb with the verb.

13. Next, the girls ate their food.

○ girls

Children may not distinguish between nouns and verbs.

● ate

Correct response

○ food

Children may not distinguish between nouns and verbs.

14. "We can't eat outside," said Lin's mom.

● can't

Correct response

○ outside

Children may not know what a contraction is.

○ said

Children may not know what a contraction is.

(Checking Skills continued)

15. The girls picked up their bags.

○ girls

Children may not distinguish between nouns and verbs.

● picked

Correct response

○ their

Children may not understand what a verb is.

Constructed-response Items

16. **Correct response:** *packed*

Children may not understand the difference between present tense and past tense verbs, or they may not have understood the instructions.

17. **Correct response:** *walked*

Children may not understand the difference between present tense and past tense verbs, or they may not have understood the instructions.

18. **Correct response:** *played*

Children may not understand the difference between present tense and past tense verbs, or they may not have understood the instructions.

19. **Correct response:** *pets, pets*

Children may not understand the concept of categorizing similar, but different, items in the same group.

20. **Correct response:** *first, now*

Children may not understand sequence and may reverse the order of the words *now* and *first* in the sentences.

Suggested Remediation: Work with children to review past and present verbs, contractions, words that define by categorizing, and sequence words. Give examples of each. Have children name actions you perform. Write sentences describing your actions on the board. Have children help you use sequence words to order the actions. Ask volunteers to underline the verbs.

WORD ANALYSIS (Recommended Time: 20–30 minutes, uninterrupted)

Teacher Directions: Have children turn to page 15. Use the following directions to administer the assessment. Read the words and sentences aloud more than once if needed. Be sure to pause after each question so that children have time to mark their answers.

(Word Analysis continued)

Tell children:

Now we are going to match the pictures to the words on the page. Listen carefully. You will decide which word goes with the picture.

21. Put your finger on the picture at the top of the page. What do you see in the picture? Next, look at the three words. Does that picture show *a ship* . . . *a sink* . . . or *a shark?* Fill in the circle under the word you chose.

22. Look at the second picture. Does that picture show *a firefighter* . . . *a fire truck* . . . or *a campfire*? Fill in the circle under the word you chose.

23. Point to the third picture. What does it show? Does the picture show *a store* . . . *a stare* . . . or *a sort?* Fill in the circle under the word you chose.

Turn to page 16.

24. Look at the first picture. Does that picture show *a wheel* . . . *a wagon* . . . or a dog *wagging* its tail? Fill in the circle next to the word you choose.

25. Look at the second picture. Does that picture show *a bed* . . . *a bird* . . . or *a burn?* Fill in the circle next to the word you choose.

Look at page 17. Now I am going to read you some sentences. Follow along in your book. I want you to circle the plural nouns that end in *-es* in the sentences. Remember, you are only circling plural nouns that end in *-es*.

26. Cups and glasses are dishes. *Cups, glasses,* and *dishes* are all plural nouns. Circle the plural nouns that end in *-es*.

27. Foxes live in dens. *Foxes* and *dens* are plural nouns. Circle the plural noun that ends in *-es*.

28. Do we need passes to get on the buses? *Passes* and *buses* are plural nouns. Circle the plural nouns that end in *-es*.

Now turn to page 18. I am going to read you sentences. Follow along in your book. Write the verb that completes each sentence.

29. I was __________ like a little bird. Which verb completes the sentence? Is it *hop* . . . *hopped* . . . or *hopping?* Write the word on the line.

30. Dad __________ the pages as he read to me. Which verb completes the sentence? Is it *turn* . . . *turned* . . . or *turning*? Write the word on the line.

<u>**Scoring:**</u> Photocopy and use the evaluation chart to track children's scores and progress.

<u>**Word Analysis Answer Key with Interpretation:**</u>

21. **Correct answer:** *sink*

Children may have chosen *ship* because they did not hear the sound /ngk/.

Children may have chosen *shark* because they did not hear the sound /ngk/.

(Word Analysis continued)

22. **Correct answer:** *campfire*

    Children may have chosen *firefighter* or *fire truck* because they heard only the *fire* part of the compound word.

23. **Correct answer:** *store*

    Children may have chosen *stare* because they cannot distinguish between the vowel sound in words with *-are* and the vowel sound in words with *-ore*.

    Children may have chosen *sort* because they heard only the /ôr/ sound.

24. **Correct answer:** *wagging*

    Children may have chosen *wheel* because they did not understand the concept of adding an inflected ending.

    Children may have chosen *wagon* because they could not distinguish the final sound of the final syllable.

25. **Correct answer:** *bird*

    Children may have chosen *bed* because they did not listen carefully to the vowel sound.

    Children may have chosen *burn* because they did not listen carefully to the final sound in the word.

26. **Correct response:** circle *glasses, dishes*

    Children may have circled all plurals.

27. **Correct response:** circle *foxes*

    Children may have circled all plurals.

28. **Correct response:** circle: *passes, buses*

    Children may have circled words other than plural nouns that end in *-es*.

29. **Correct response:** *hopping*

    Children may have chosen the present form of the word or may not understand inflected endings.

30. **Correct response:** *turned*

    Children may have chosen the present form of the word or may not understand inflected endings.

Suggested Remediation: Review the long vowel patterns, *r*-controlled vowels, long vowels *e* and *i* spelled *y*, consonant patterns /ngk/ and /ng/, inflected forms, and plurals ending in *-s* and *-es*. Have children brainstorm lists of words with the same consonant or vowel patterns. Write the words on the board and ask children to circle the vowel or consonant patterns. Give children lists of words to make plural. Discuss why some words form the plural with *-es* whereas others use *-s*. Have children write inflected forms of words using *-ed* and *-ing*. Discuss the use of each inflected form.

VOCABULARY (Recommended Time: 20–30 minutes, uninterrupted)

<u>**Teacher Directions:**</u> Have children look at page 19. Use the following directions to administer the assessment.

Read the following directions to children:

Now we will choose pictures that match sentences.

31. Read the sentence *The girl stands.* Look at the three pictures. Which picture shows what happens in the sentence *The girl stands?* Fill in the circle below the picture you chose.

32. Read the sentence *The sky is cloudy today.* Look at the three pictures. Which picture shows what happens in the sentence *The sky is cloudy today*? Fill in the circle below the picture you chose.

Now turn to page 20. Look at the pictures. I will say a sentence that talks about one of the pictures you see in your book. Fill in the circle next to the correct word.

33. Here is the sentence: *You live in this place, especially with your family.* Now, which picture matches this sentence best? *You live in this place, especially with your family.* Fill in the circle next to the word you chose.

34. Here is the next sentence: *These animals have long necks and are related to ducks.* Now, which picture matches this sentence best? *These animals have long necks and are related to ducks.* Fill in the circle next to the word you chose.

35. Here is the next sentence: *This vehicle has two wheels that you sit on and ride.* Now, which picture matches this sentence best? *This vehicle has two wheels that you sit on and ride.* Fill in the circle next to the word you chose.

Look at page 21. I will read you a question. You will write the answer. Your answer can be one word. Write the word on the line. Listen carefully.

36. Look at the picture at the top of the page. *What direction is the opposite of north?*

37. Look at the next picture. *What is the season between winter and summer?*

38. Look at the next picture. *What do we call the temperature and state of conditions, like wind, rain, sun?*

39. There is no picture for this question. **Listen carefully. *Which word means "each one"?***

40. There is no picture for this question. **Listen carefully. *Which word means "belonging to us"?***

<u>**Scoring:**</u> Photocopy and use the evaluation chart to track children's scores and progress.

(Vocabulary continued)

Key: Vocabulary Answer Key with Interpretation

31. The girl **stands.**

Correct answer: first picture

Children may choose the second picture showing the girl before she stands. They may not understand the word *stands*.

Children who chose the third picture may not understand the meaning of *stands*.

32. The sky is **cloudy** today.

Children who chose the first picture may be focusing on the word *sky.* They may not understand the word *cloudy.*

Correct answer: second picture

Children who chose the third picture may be focusing on the word *sky.* They may not understand the word *cloudy.*

33. **Correct response:** *house*

Children may have chosen *school* or *building* because they did not listen carefully and heard only a place mentioned.

34. **Correct response:** *geese*

Children may have chosen *birds* because they heard the word *ducks*, and ducks are birds.

Children may have chosen *spring* because they did not listen carefully or did not understand the sentence.

(Vocabulary continued)

35. **Correct response:** *bicycle*

    Children may have chosen *car* because they focused on the word *vehicle*.

    Children may have chosen *wheels* because they focused on the *two wheels* mentioned in the sentence.

36. **Correct response:** *south*

    The correct answer is the vocabulary word *south*. If children write another word, such as *east* or *west*, they understand the concept of direction but do not realize which direction is opposite of north. If children write a word that does not make sense as an answer to the question, they may not understand some of the words in the definition.

37. **Correct response:** *spring*

    The correct answer is the vocabulary word *spring.* If children write another word, such as *fall* or *summer*, they understand the concept of seasons but do not realize which season comes between winter and summer. If children write a word that does not make sense as an answer to the question, they may not understand some of the words in the definition.

38. **Correct response:** *weather*

    The correct answer is the vocabulary word *weather*. If children write another word, such as *rain* or *cloudy*, they understand the concept of weather but do not know the difference between the overall concept of *weather* and individual weather types. If children write a word that does not make sense as an answer to the question, they may not understand some of the words in the definition.

39. **Correct response:** *every*

    The correct answer is the vocabulary word *every.* If children write another word such as *each* or *one,* they understand part of the concept but are just answering part of the question. If children write a word that does not make sense as an answer to the question, they may not understand some of the words in the definition.

(Vocabulary continued)

40. **Correct response:** *our*

The correct answer is the vocabulary word *our*. If children write another word such as *mine*, they understand the concept of possession but do not understand the concept of plural. If children write a word that does not make sense as an answer to the question, they may not understand some of the words in the definition.

Suggested Remediation: Review the multiple-choice sentences. Discuss all the information provided in the sentences. Then help children identify the answer that best fits the information. Discuss the multiple-choice pictures and all the information provided in each sentence. Then help children identify the answer that best fits the information. Review the unit's vocabulary with children. Use word and definition cards. Have children draw a picture on the word card to help with identification. Then have children match the word cards with their definition cards.

WRITING (Recommended Time: 15–20 minutes, uninterrupted)

Teacher Directions: Have children turn to page 22. Make sure they have pencils. Read the prompt aloud and point out the illustration on page 23. Make sure children know to draw their picture on page 24 and write their response on page 25. Then read through the writing checklist on page 27. You may wish to give children scrap paper to use to plan their writing, or permit them to use page 26 as scrap paper.

Read the following directions to children:

For the last part of the test, you will draw a picture and write at least two sentences about a topic I'm about to read to you. The topic explains what you are going to draw and write about. The topic also gives you some ideas for planning.

If you do not know how to spell a word, sound out the word and do the best you can. Write as neatly as you can. Be sure your sentences are about the topic. Here is the topic you should draw and write about:

(Writing continued)

Prompt:

> In "Rainy Day Picnic," Lin and her friends wanted to eat outside. It rained, so the girls changed their plans. Tell about a time you changed your plans. What did you want to do? Why did you change plans? Then tell what you did do. Draw a picture showing a time you changed plans. Then write at least two sentences about it.

Point out the picture of Lin and her friends eating lunch inside a park building on page 23. Read the caption: **Here is what happened when Lin and her friends had to change plans.** Point out the drawing box on page 24 and the lines on page 25 for writing.

Then point out the checklist on page 27.

Here are some things to remember when you are drawing and writing:
Did you draw a picture showing a time you changed plans?
Did you think about a time when you had to change your plans?
Did you tell what you wanted to do, and what you did do?
Do your sentences make sense?
Do your sentences begin with a capital letter?
Do your sentences end with a punctuation mark?
Remember to look at your drawing.
Remember to write at least two complete sentences.
Remember to reread your sentences.

Now think about what you would like to draw and write. You have 20 minutes. Remember to ask yourself the questions on page 27 after you are finished working. Make sure you write at least two complete sentences.

Be sure to answer any questions children may have. Read the prompt a second time. Alert them when they have five minutes remaining.

Scoring: See page vii of this manual for information on how to score Writing.

(Writing continued)

5-Point Scoring Rubric

5	4	3	2	1
• writing is well focused on topic	• writing is focused on topic	• writing is mostly focused on topic	• writing is generally focused on topic	• writing is not focused on topic
• idea is very clear	• idea is clear	• idea is mostly clear	• idea is generally clear	• idea is unclear
• sentences are complete	• sentences are mostly complete	• sentences are mostly complete	• sentences are incomplete	• writes only one sentence; incomplete
• excellent use of writing conventions	• very good use of writing conventions	• good use of writing conventions	• frequent errors in writing conventions	• shows serious errors in writing conventions

Sample Responses:

Possible response (5-point score):

Dad and I wanted to go sledding. The snow melted. We went on a hike.

Possible response (4-point score):

We plan to ride bikes. It rains. We stay home.

Possible response (3-point score):

I call Ben. He sick and can't play. I call Pete.

Possible response (2-point score):

A big storm. No Lights. We tell stories.

Possible response (1-point score):

Me sleep to lat. I mis it.

FLUENCY (Time: 5–10 minutes preparation; 1 minute per student for reading)

Teacher Directions: Please refer to the "General Directions for the Administration of the Oral Reading Fluency Assessment" in this Teacher's Manual. Make enough copies of the following pages for each student. Do not provide students with a copy until test time.

Name ______________________________ Date ______________

Unit 3 Fluency

Teacher Copy

Say these specific directions to the student:

When I say "Begin," start reading aloud at the top of this page. Read across the page (DEMONSTRATE BY POINTING). *Try to read each word. If you come to a word you don't know, I will say the word for you. Read as quickly and accurately as you can, but do not read SO fast that you make mistakes. Do your best reading.*

A New Pal

I hopped into bed.	4
Dad was tucking me in.	9
"Wait," I said. "I need Pal."	15
Pal is my blue and yellow bird.	22
I always take Pal to bed.	28
Dad looked under the bed.	33
I looked in the box.	38
We couldn't find Pal. He was lost.	45
"What can we do?" I said. "I need Pal."	54
I wanted to cry.	58
Then Dad said, "I will be back soon."	66
Dad came back with a big dog.	73
"This was my pal," said Dad.	79
"You can have him."	83
I grinned as Dad gave me his pal.	91
Dad tucked us in. Then Dad read to us.	100

EVALUATING CODES FOR ORAL READING

~~sky~~	(/)	word read incorrectly
blue ^ sky	(^)	inserted word
	(])	after the last word read

Comments:

FLUENCY SCORE

Number of Words Read per Minute: ________

Number of Errors ________

Number of Words Read Correctly: ________

Errors include: 1) words read incorrectly; 2) words left out or inserted; 3) mispronounced words; 4) dropped endings or sounds; and 5) reversals. Self corrections and word repetitions are NOT marked as errors.

Name ______________________________ Date ____________________

Unit 3 Fluency

Student Copy

A New Pal

I hopped into bed.

Dad was tucking me in.

"Wait," I said. "I need Pal."

Pal is my blue and yellow bird.

I always take Pal to bed.

Dad looked under the bed.

I looked in the box.

We couldn't find Pal. He was lost.

"What can we do?" I said. "I need Pal."

I wanted to cry.

Then Dad said, "I will be back soon."

Dad came back with a big dog.

"This was my pal," said Dad.

"You can have him."

I grinned as Dad gave me his pal.

Dad tucked us in. Then Dad read to us.

Unit 3 Test Evaluation Chart

Name ______________________________ Date ____________

Item	Skill	Week/Day	Item/Type*	Assistance (circle)	Score (circle one)
1	Plot	Week 2 Day 3	MC	Y N	0 1 2
2	Sequence	Week 1 Day 3	MC	Y N	0 1 2
3	Plot	Week 2 Day 3	MC	Y N	0 1 2
4	Plot	Week 2 Day 3	MC	Y N	0 1 2
5	Sequence	Week 4 Day 3	MC	Y N	0 1 2
6	Steps in a Process	Week 6 Day 3	MC	Y N	0 1 2
7	Steps in a Process	Week 6 Day 3	MC	Y N	0 1 2
8	Steps in a Process	Week 6 Day 3	MC	Y N	0 1 2
9	Steps in a Process	Week 6 Day 3	MC	Y N	0 1 2
10	Steps in a Process	Week 6 Day 3	MC	Y N	0 1 2
11	Sequence Words	Week 4 Day 3	MC	Y N	0 1 2
12	Verbs	Week 1 Day 4	MC	Y N	0 1 2
13	Action Verbs	Week 1 Day 4	MC	Y N	0 1 2
14	Contractions with Not	Week 6 Day 4	MC	Y N	0 1 2
15	Verbs for Past and Present	Week 4 Day 4	MC	Y N	0 1 2
16	Verbs for Past and Present	Week 4 Day 4	CR	Y N	0 1 2
17	Verbs for Past and Present	Week 4 Day 4	CR	Y N	0 1 2
18	Verbs for Past and Present	Week 4 Day 4	CR	Y N	0 1 2
19	Classify and Categorize	Week 5 Day 3	CR	Y N	0 1 2
20	Sequencing	Week 1 Day 3	CR	Y N	0 1 2
21	/ngk/ Spelled *nk*	Week 2 Day 2	MC	Y N	0 1 2
22	Compound Words	Week 2 Day 2	MC	Y N	0 1 2
23	/ôr/ spelled *or*	Week 3 Day 2	MC	Y N	0 1 2
24	Inflected Endings	Week 4 Day 2	MC	Y N	0 1 2
25	/ėr/ Spelled *ir*	Week 5 Day 2	MC	Y N	0 1 2
26	Plural *-es*	Week 3 Day 2	CR	Y N	0 1 2
27	Plural *-es*	Week 3 Day 2	CR	Y N	0 1 2
28	Plural *-es*	Week 3 Day 2	CR	Y N	0 1 2
29	Inflected Endings *-ed, -ing*	Week 4 Day 2	CR	Y N	0 1 2
30	Inflected Endings *-ed, -ing*	Week 4 Day 2	CR	Y N	0 1 2
31	Vocabulary	Week 1 Day 1	MC	Y N	0 1 2
32	Vocabulary	Week 4 Day 1	MC	Y N	0 1 2
33	Vocabulary	Week 1 Day 1	MC	Y N	0 1 2
34	Vocabulary	Week 5 Day 1	MC	Y N	0 1 2
35	Vocabulary	Week 2 Day 1	MC	Y N	0 1 2
36	Vocabulary	Week 6 Day 1	CR	Y N	0 1 2
37	Vocabulary	Week 5 Day 1	CR	Y N	0 1 2
38	Vocabulary	Week 4 Day 1	CR	Y N	0 1 2
39	Vocabulary	Week 2 Day 1	CR	Y N	0 1 2
40	Vocabulary	Week 3 Day 1	CR	Y N	0 1 2
SCORE A: Skills and Content					____ out of 80
SCORE B: Writing				Y N	2 4 6 8 10
SCORE C: Fluency				WCPM ______	2 4 6 8 10
OVERALL SCORE					____ out of 100

*MC = multiple choice CR = constructed respons

Grade 1, Unit 4
Answer Key and Directions

COMPREHENSION (Recommended Time: 30–45 minutes, uninterrupted)

Teacher Directions: Directions in **bold** are to be read aloud; others are for your information only. Use the following directions to administer the assessment. Make sure all children have a test booklet copy and pencils, and that children are on page 2 of the booklet. Explain that they will listen to a story and then answer some questions about it. Have students look at the picture and follow along as you read. Be sure to pause after each question so that children have time to mark their answers.

Read the following to the children:

Now I'm going to read a story about Felix, his neighbors, and a party. After the first part of the story, I will ask you some questions. Listen carefully. The story is called "Happy Birthday, America!" Here is the first part of the story.

Happy Birthday, America!

1 **Felix looked at the calendar.**

2 **There was a big, red circle around July 4.**

3 **Felix and his family were having a birthday party for the United States.**

Look at the next page.

4 **Felix sent cards to the neighbors.**

5 **Ana hung red, white, and blue banners on the gate.**

6 **Dad set up a big table in the yard.**

Turn to page 4.

7 **Mom made tacos.**

8 **Ana put tomatoes on a plate.**

9 **Jack roasted corn on the grill.**

10 **Mr. Lee made a rice dish.**

11 **Mrs. Lee brought fruit.**

Now model how to fill in the circle. Demonstrate the directions to the students, using a student test book. Read each question twice.

(Comprehension continued)

Tell the children:

Now look at page 5. I am going to ask you some questions about this part of the story. For each question that I ask, you will see three pictures in a row. Ask yourself which picture goes with the question I ask. Fill in the circle below the picture that shows the best answer. Listen carefully.

1. **Look at the first row of pictures at the top of the page. How did Felix tell the neighbors about the party? Did he *tell them when he sees them . . . call them on the phone* ...... or *mail them cards*? Put your finger on the picture that shows how Felix told his neighbors about the party. Then fill in the circle below the picture you chose.**
2. **Point to the next row of pictures. What were the neighbors doing? Were the neighbors at *a picnic . . . a zoo* . . . or *a mall?* Fill in the circle below the picture that shows the best answer.**
3. **Move down to the next row of pictures. Where was the party? Was the party in *the classroom . . . the backyard* . . . or *the kitchen?* Fill in the circle below the picture that shows the best answer.**

Ask children to turn to page 6.

4. **Look at the top row of pictures. How did Felix know the date for the party? Did Felix look at *a calendar . . . a flag* . . . or *a clock?* Fill in the circle below the picture that shows the best answer.**
5. **Look down at the next row of pictures. What did Dad do before the neighbors came? Did Dad *set up the table . . . hang banners* . . . or *slice tomatoes?* Fill in the circle below the picture that shows the best answer.**

Look at page 7. Now I am going to read the second part of the story. Then I will ask you some more questions. Listen carefully. Here is the rest of the story.

Happy Birthday, America! (part 2)

12 **Grandpa told stories about when he was a little boy.**

13 **Grandpa lived on a small farm in Mexico.**

14 **Mr. Lee showed pictures of the city in China where he grew up.**

Now turn to page 8.

15 **The neighbors went to the Fourth of July parade.**

16 **They saw marching bands.**

17 **They waved flags.**

18 **Soon it was dark.**

19 **But the party was not over.**

20 **Bright fireworks filled the sky.**

21 **Felix was glad to celebrate this special day.**

(Comprehension continued)

Now the story about America's birthday is over, and I will ask you more questions. Look at page 9.

6. **Look at the first row of pictures. What were the neighbors celebrating? Were they celebrating *the Fourth of July . . . a graduation . . . or winning a race?* Put your finger on the picture that shows what the neighbors were celebrating. Then fill in the circle below that picture.**

7. **Move down to the next row of pictures. What did the neighbors see at the parade? Did they see *fireworks . . . a marching band* . . . or *a lady on a horse?* Fill in the circle below the picture that shows what the neighbors saw at the parade.**

8. **Point to the next row of pictures. What did Felix see in the sky? Did he see *rain clouds . . . fireworks* . . . or *a rainbow?* Fill in the circle below the picture you chose.**

Ask children to turn to page 10.

For each of these two questions, you will see three pictures and a word for each picture. Fill in the circle below the picture and word that best answer the question.

9. **Where did Grandpa live when he was a little boy? Did Grandpa live *in an apartment . . . in a house in the woods* . . . or *on a farm?* Fill in the circle below the word that you choose.**

10. **How did Felix feel at the end of the day? Did Felix feel *mad . . . happy . . . or sad?* Fill in the circle below the word that you choose.**

<u>Scoring</u>: Photocopy and use the evaluation chart to track children's scores and progress.

<u>Comprehension Answer Key with Interpretation:</u>

1. How did Felix tell the neighbors about the party?

○ ○ ●

Children who chose the first picture (child waving) may not have noted that Felix sent cards.

Children who chose the second picture (boy on telephone) may have selected it because the telephone is a familiar form of communication.

Correct answer: third picture (boy mailing cards)

(Comprehension continued)

2. What were the neighbors doing?

Correct answer: first picture (picnic)

Children who chose the second picture (zoo) may have selected it because it shows people in an outdoor setting.

Children who chose the third picture (people at a mall) may have selected it because it shows a large group of people.

3. Where was the party?

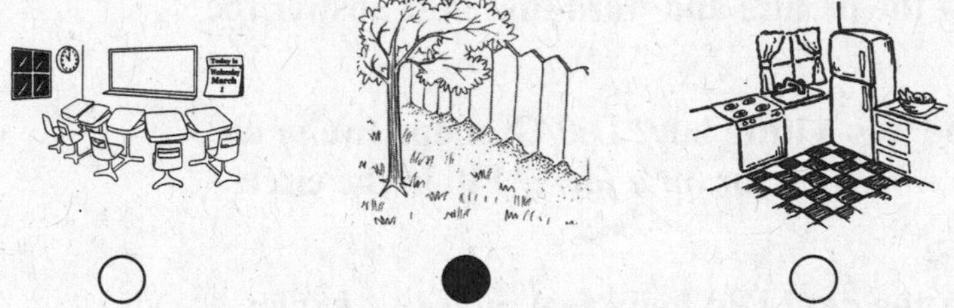

Children who chose the first picture (a classroom) may have selected it because a classroom can accommodate a large group of people.

Correct answer: second picture (a backyard)

Children who chose the third picture (a kitchen) may have selected it because the kitchen is a usual gathering place.

4. How did Felix know the date for the party?

Correct answer: first picture (a calendar)

Children who chose the second picture (a flag) may have thought the question was asking what the party was for.

Children who chose the third picture (clock) may not distinguish between instruments for measuring date/time.

(Comprehension continued)

5. What did Dad do before the neighbors came?

Correct answer: first picture (man setting up a table)

Children who chose the second picture (man hanging banners) may have selected it because the banners were put up before the neighbors came.

Children who chose the third picture (man slicing tomatoes) may not recall details of the story.

6. What were the neighbors celebrating?

Correct answer: first picture (the Fourth of July)

Children who chose the second picture (girl graduating) may have selected it because the celebration was outdoors.

Children who chose the third picture (winning a race) may have selected it because the celebration was outdoors.

7. What did the neighbors see at the parade?

Children who chose the first picture (fireworks) may have selected it because fireworks are mentioned in the story.

Correct answer: second picture (marching band)

Children who chose the third picture (lady on a horse) may have selected it because performers like her often appear in parades.

(Comprehension continued)

8. What did Felix see in the sky?

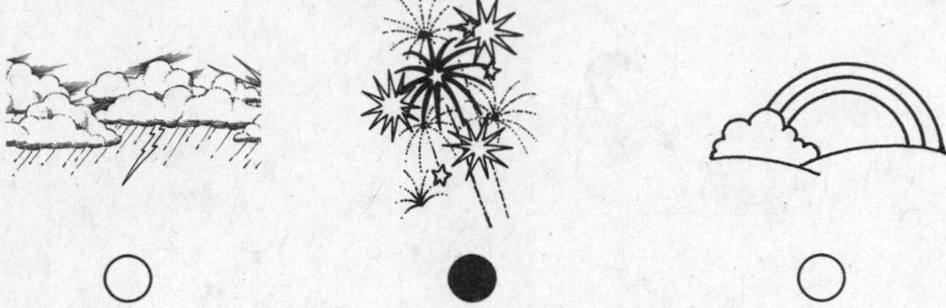

Children who chose the first picture (rain clouds) may have selected it because clouds can be seen in the sky.

Correct answer: second picture (fireworks)

Children who chose the third picture (rainbow) may have selected it because a rainbow can be bright and colorful like fireworks.

9. Where did Grandpa live when he was a little boy?

Children who chose the first picture (apartment) may have selected it because an apartment is a familiar type of housing.

Children who chose the second picture (a house in the woods) may not distinguish between the setting of the story and where Grandpa lived when he was a little boy.

Correct answer: third picture (farm)

10. How did Felix feel at the end of the day?

Children who chose the first picture (boy scowling) did not connect the story text with picture clues.

Correct answer: second picture (boy smiling)

Children who chose the third picture (boy crying) may have selected it because the party was over at the end of the day.

(Comprehension continued)

<u>**Suggested Remediation**</u>: Discuss each part of the story, using the pictures and words to identify the main ideas and details. Discuss what each family member did to help with the party, for example. Reread the story with children and model how to draw conclusions.

CHECKING SKILLS (Recommended Time: 20 minutes, uninterrupted)

<u>**Teacher Directions:**</u> Use the following directions to administer the assessment. Read the sentences aloud more than once if needed. Be sure to pause after each question so that children have time to mark their answers. Make sure all children are on page 11 before you begin.

Now I am going to read some incomplete sentences to you. The sentences I will read tell about the story "Happy Birthday, America!" Pick the word that goes with what I read. Listen carefully.

11. Look at the picture at the top of the page. Here is the sentence: *The band marched* ________. Which word—*sadly, kindly,* or *slowly*—best completes the sentence? Point to that word. Fill in the circle below the word.

12. Put your finger next to the second picture. Here is the sentence: *The man* ________ *bread.* Which word—*baked, skipped,* or *jumped*—best completes the sentence? Fill in the circle below the word.

13. Look at the next picture. Here is the sentence: *Mom patted the baby* ________. Which word—*loudly, softly,* or *shortly*—best completes the sentence? Fill in the circle below the word.

Now turn to page 12.

14. Look at the picture at the top of the page. Here is the sentence: *Felix* ________ *the card.* Which word—*mailed, surprised,* or *tossed*—best completes the sentence? Fill in the circle below the word.

15. Look at the next picture. Here is the sentence: *Jack* ________ *with his mom.* Which word—*jumped, snapped,* or *laughed*—best completes the sentence? Fill in the circle below the word.

Look at page 13. Now we are going to look at pictures. You will write a sentence about each picture. Write your sentences on the lines.

16. Look at the picture at the top of the page. It shows a boy, a cat, and a tree. On the lines, write a sentence about the cat. Use an adjective in your sentence.

17. Look at the next picture. It shows a girl with a pencil and paper. On the lines, write a sentence about the picture. Use an adjective in your sentence.

18. Look at the next picture. It shows two children who have blocks. On the lines, write a sentence about the picture. Use an adjective in your sentence.

(Checking Skills continued)

Now turn to page 14.

Now we are going to look at pairs of pictures. I will read an incomplete sentence about the pictures to you. You will write a word to complete the sentence. Write your word on the line.

19. Look at the pictures at the top of the page. They show two kinds of fruit. Here is the sentence: *The watermelon is ________ than the apple.* On the line, write a comparing adjective to complete the sentence.

20. Look at the next picture. It shows two animals. Here is the sentence: *The mouse is ________ than the elephant.* On the line, write a comparing adjective to complete the sentence.

<u>Scoring</u>: Photocopy and use the evaluation chart to track children's scores and progress.

<u>Checking Skills Answer Key with Interpretation:</u>

11. The band marched ________.

○ sadly

Children may have chosen the first word *(sadly)* because they do not know the meaning of the root word *sad.*

○ kindly

Children may have chosen the second word *(kindly)* because they do not know the meaning of the root word *kind.*

● slowly

Correct answer: third word *(slowly)*

12. The man ________ bread.

● baked

Correct answer: first word *(baked)*

○ skipped

Children may have chosen the second word *(skipped)* because they do not know the meaning of the root word *skip.*

○ jumped

Children may have chosen the third word *(jumped)* because they do not know the meaning of the root word *jump.*

(Checking Skills continued)

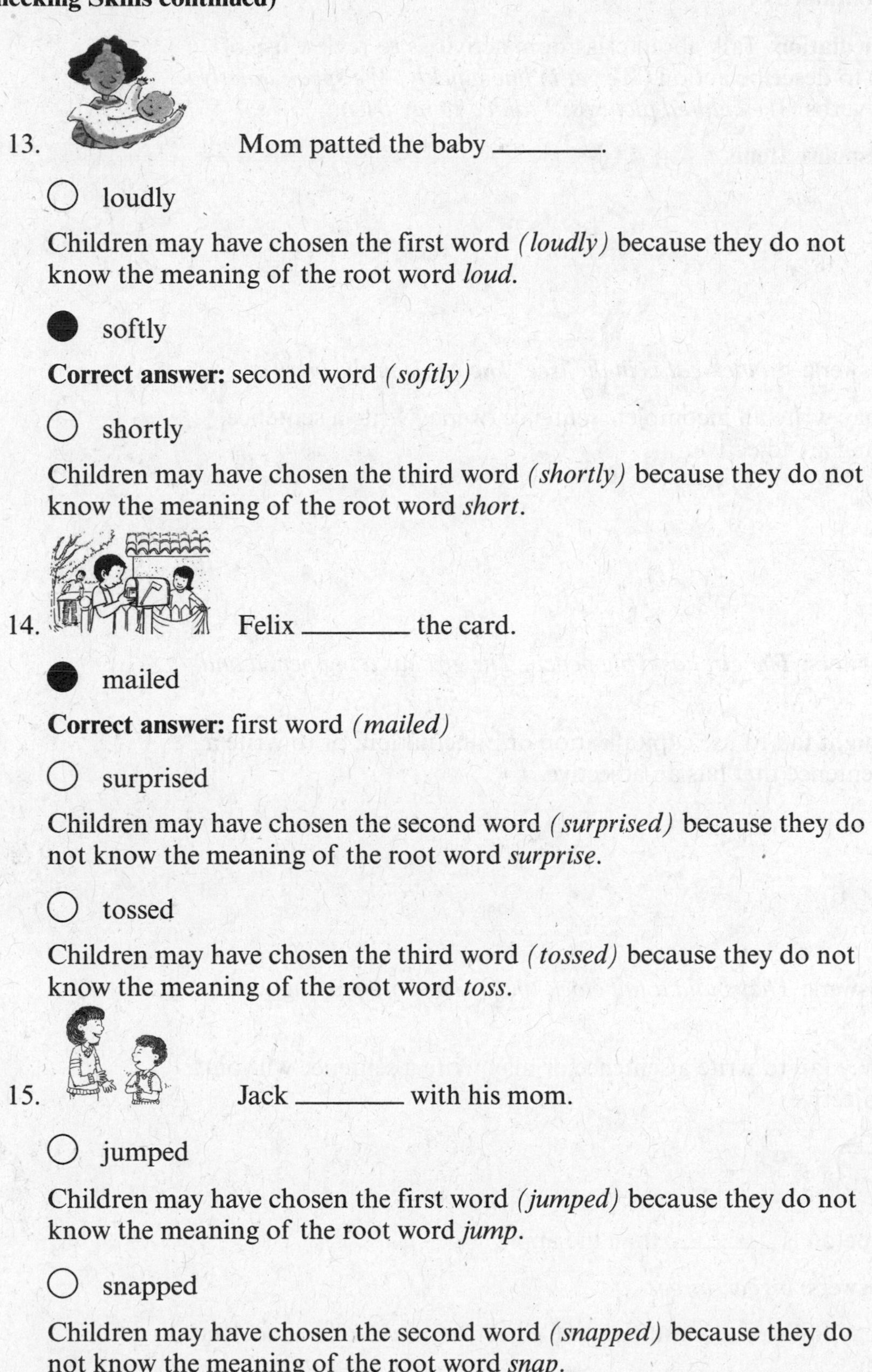

13. Mom patted the baby ________.

○ loudly

Children may have chosen the first word *(loudly)* because they do not know the meaning of the root word *loud.*

● softly

Correct answer: second word *(softly)*

○ shortly

Children may have chosen the third word *(shortly)* because they do not know the meaning of the root word *short*.

14. Felix ________ the card.

● mailed

Correct answer: first word *(mailed)*

○ surprised

Children may have chosen the second word *(surprised)* because they do not know the meaning of the root word *surprise*.

○ tossed

Children may have chosen the third word *(tossed)* because they do not know the meaning of the root word *toss*.

15. Jack ________ with his mom.

○ jumped

Children may have chosen the first word *(jumped)* because they do not know the meaning of the root word *jump*.

○ snapped

Children may have chosen the second word *(snapped)* because they do not know the meaning of the root word *snap*.

● laughed

Correct answer: third word *(laughed)*

(**Checking Skills continued**)

Suggested Remediation: Talk about classroom activities to review use of words with *–ly* to describe action (*We get in line quickly; We speak quietly*) and past tense verbs (*We colored pictures; I talked to my friends*).

Constructed-response Items

16. 

Possible answers: *A black cat is in the tree. The cat is in the big tree.*

Children may write an incomplete sentence or may write a sentence without using an adjective.

17. 

Possible answers: *The girl has a big pencil. The girl has a big pencil and long paper.*

Children might fail to use capitalization or punctuation, or to write a complete sentence that has an adjective.

18. 

Possible answers: *They build a tall block tower. They are playing with square blocks.*

Children may fail to write a sentence or may write a sentence without using an adjective.

19. 

The watermelon is ________ than the apple.

Possible answers: *bigger, larger*

Children may fail to use a comparative adjective or make an incorrect comparison.

(Checking Skills continued)

20.  The mouse is ______ than the elephant.
Possible answer: *smaller*

Possible answers: *smaller, littler*

Children may fail to use a comparative adjective or make an incorrect comparison.

Suggested Remediation: Have students take turns using adjectives to describe and compare common classroom objects. Have students point to objects as they use adjectives and make comparisons, e.g., *a big book, a bigger book, the biggest book.*

WORD ANALYSIS (Recommended Time: 20–30 minutes, uninterrupted)

Teacher Directions: Have the children turn to page 15. Use the following directions to administer the assessment. Read the words and sentences aloud more than once if needed. Be sure to pause after each question so that children have time to mark their answers.

Now we are going to match the pictures to the words. Listen carefully. I'm going to say a word that names the picture. Look at the words in your book. Choose the word that you heard. You may say the word aloud before you decide.

21. Put your finger on the picture at the top of the page. The picture shows a sail. The word is *sail.* Look at the three words. Fill in the circle below the word *sail.*

22. Look at the second picture. The picture shows a bean. The word is *bean.* Look at the three words. Fill in the circle below the word *bean.*

23. Point to the third picture. The picture shows a coat. The word is *coat.* Look at the three words. Fill in the circle below the word *coat.*

Turn to page 16.

Now we are going to match the pictures to compound words. Look at the picture. Look at the words written in your book. Choose the word that names the picture. You may say the words aloud before you decide.

24. Look at the picture at the top of the page. What does the picture show? Look at the three words. Fill in the circle next to the compound word that names the picture.

25. Look at the next picture. What does the picture show? Look at the three words. Fill in the circle next to the compound word that names the picture.

Look at page 17. Now we will study words. This time you will decide what vowel sound a word makes. Then you will write a word that makes the same vowel sound.

26. Look at the picture at the top of the page. The picture shows a spoon. The word is *spoon.* Write a word that has the same vowel sound as the word *spoon.*

(Word Analysis continued)

27. Look at the next picture. The picture shows juice. The word is *juice.* Write a word that has the same vowel sound as the word *juice.*

28. Move on to the next picture. The picture shows a leaf. The word is *leaf.* Write a word that has the same vowel sound as the word *leaf.*

Now turn to page 18.

29. Look at the picture at the top of the page. The picture shows a knob. The word is *knob.* Write a word that has the same vowel sound as the word *knob.*

30. Look at the next picture. The picture shows writing. The word is *write.* Write a word that has the same vowel sound as the word *write.*

Scoring: Photocopy and use the evaluation chart to track children's scores and progress.

Key: Word Analysis Answer Key with Interpretation:

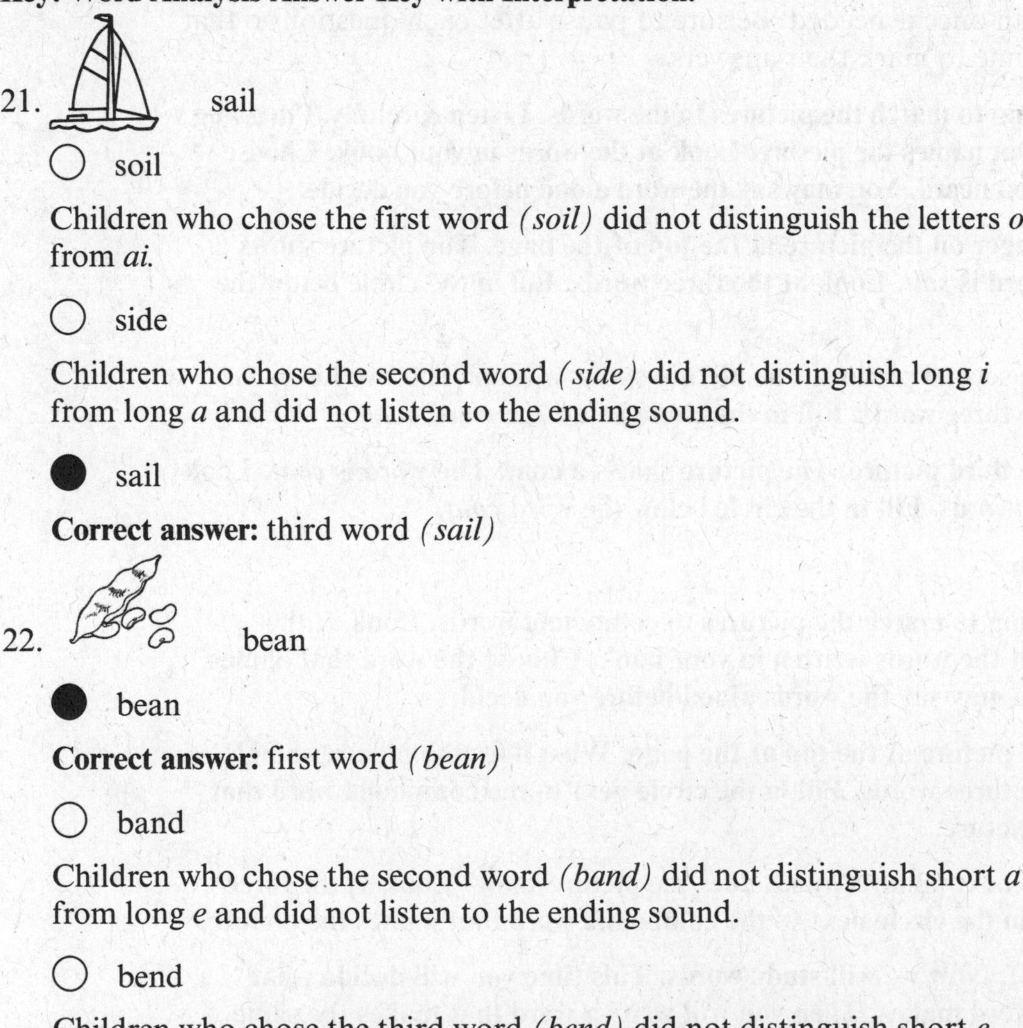

21. sail

○ soil

Children who chose the first word *(soil)* did not distinguish the letters *oi* from *ai.*

○ side

Children who chose the second word *(side)* did not distinguish long *i* from long *a* and did not listen to the ending sound.

● sail

Correct answer: third word *(sail)*

22. bean

● bean

Correct answer: first word *(bean)*

○ band

Children who chose the second word *(band)* did not distinguish short *a* from long *e* and did not listen to the ending sound.

○ bend

Children who chose the third word *(bend)* did not distinguish short *e* from long *e* and did not listen to the ending sound.

(Word Analysis continued)

23. coat

○ cane

Children who chose the first word *(cane)* did not distinguish long *a* from long *o* and did not listen to the ending sound.

● coat

Correct answer: second word *(coat)*

○ cot

Children who chose the third word *(cot)* did not distinguish short *o* from long *o*.

<u>**Suggested Remediation**</u>: To help children identify sound/symbol correspondences, have children work with a partner to identify and sort picture cards according to the medial sounds. Then help children relate sounds to letters.

24.

○ footstep

Children who chose the first word *(footstep)* did not make the connection between the compound word and picture clues.

○ rainbow

Children who chose the second word *(rainbow)* did not make the connection between the compound word and picture clues.

● snowman

Correct compound word *(snowman)*

25.

○ doorbell

Children who chose the first word *(doorbell)* did not make the connection between the compound word and picture clues.

● airplane

Correct answer: second picture *(airplane)*

○ playground

Children who chose the third word *(playground)* did not make the connection between the compound word and picture clues.

(Word Analysis continued)

Suggested Remediation: To reinforce compound words, make a two-column chart on the board with the words *fire, sun,* and *bath* in column one and *place, flower,* and *tub* in column two. Have students choose one word from each column to make a compound word. Ask children to illustrate their word and share their work with other students.

26. spoon

Possible answers: *moon, loom, boom, soon, zoom, noon, room*

Children who gave other responses *(cot* or *spot)* may not have understood the long vowel sound in *spoon.*

27. juice

Possible answers: *fruit, loose, true, moose, chew, glue*

Children who gave other responses (*pull, bug,* or *drum*) may not have understood the medial vowel sound in *juice.*

28. leaf

Possible answers: *tea, flea, pea, peach, read, beak, weak, speak, deal, meal, team, clean.* Children who gave other responses *(left, fall,* or *bread)* may not have understood the long vowel sound in *leaf.*

29. knob

Possible answers: *box, pot, job, mop, top, odd*

Children who gave other responses *(snow, blow,* or *won)* may not have understood the medial vowel sound in *knob.*

30. write

Possible answers: *sight, spider, ice, cry, pie, fly*

Children who gave other responses (*rake, run,* or *rug*) may not have understood the medial vowel sound in *write.*

Suggested Remediation: Use letter cards to review sound-spelling relationships. Help students form words using each of the vowel patterns and sort them according to sounds.

VOCABULARY (Recommended Time: 20–30 minutes, uninterrupted)

Teacher Directions: Have children look at page 19. Use the following directions to administer the assessment.

Tell children:

Now we will choose pictures that match sentences.

31. Read the sentence *Ann saw the moon shining in the evening sky.* Look at the three pictures. Which picture shows something in the sentence *Ann saw the moon shining in the evening sky?* Fill in the circle below the picture you choose.

32. Read the sentence *I grew vegetables in my garden.* Look at the three pictures. Which picture shows something in the sentence *I grew vegetables in my garden?* Fill in the circle below the picture you chose.

33. Read the sentence *We gave Tom a surprise party for his birthday.* Look at the three pictures. Which picture shows something in the sentence *We gave Tom a surprise party for his birthday?* Fill in the circle below the picture you chose.

Turn to page 20.

34. Read the sentence *There was an American flag in front of the post office.* Look at the three pictures. Which picture shows something in the sentence *There was an American flag in front of the post office?* Fill in the circle below the picture you chose.

35. Read the sentence *José made a card for his mother.* Look at the three pictures. Which picture shows something in the sentence *José made a card for his mother?* Fill in the circle below the picture you chose.

Look at page 21. I will read you questions. You will write the answer. Your answer can be one word. Write the word on the line. Listen carefully.

Be sure to read the questions slowly and, if needed, more than once.

36. What do you call a nation with its land and people?

37. What do you do when you make something new?

38. What is the amount of importance that something has?

39. What do you call the people who live near you?

40. Who is the official leader of a country that does not have a king or queen?

Scoring: Photocopy and use the evaluation chart to track children scores and progress.

(Vocabulary continued)

Vocabulary Answer Key with Interpretation:

31. Ann saw the **moon** shining in the evening sky.

Children who chose the first picture *(cloud)* may have selected it because a cloud is an object in the sky.

Correct answer: second picture *(moon)*

Children who chose the third picture *(sun)* may have selected it because the sun is an object in the sky.

32. I grew vegetables in my **garden**.

Children who chose the first picture *(tree)* may have selected it because it is a plant that grows outdoors.

Children who chose the second picture *(fruit)* may have selected it because they know that fruit comes from plants.

Correct answer: third picture *(garden)*

33. We gave Tom a **surprise** party for his birthday.

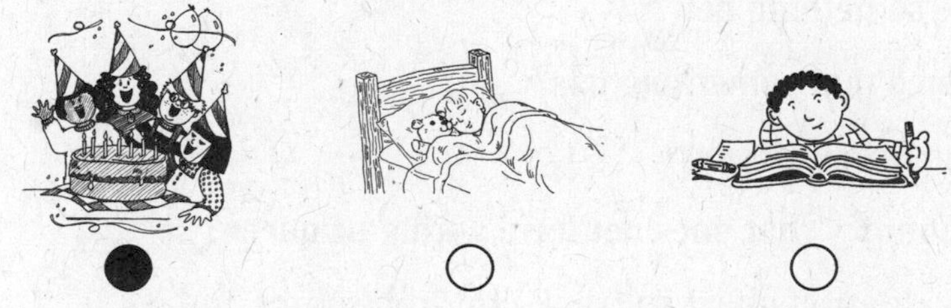

Correct answer: first picture *(surprise)*

Children who chose the second picture *(sleep)* may not know the meaning of the word *surprise.*

Children who chose the third picture *(boy doing homework)* may not distinguish the concepts of work and play.

(Vocabulary continued)

34. There was an American **flag** in front of the post office.

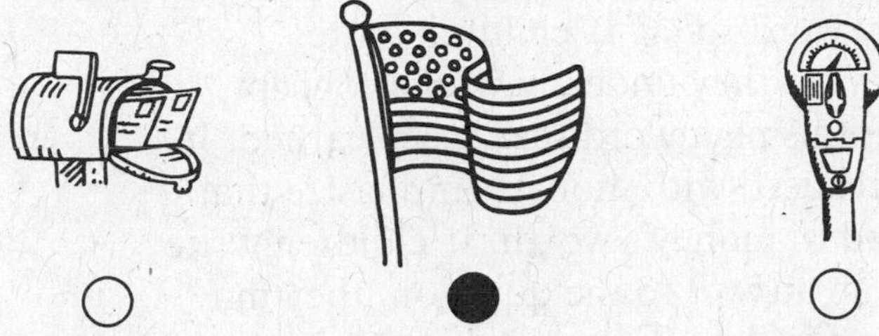

Children who chose the first picture *(mailbox)* may have selected it because of the association between mailboxes and the post office.

Correct answer: second picture *(flag)*

Children who chose the third picture *(parking mèter)* may have selected it because parking meters are a common sight on streets in front of buildings.

35. José made a **card** for his mother.

Correct answer: first picture *(card)*

Children who chose the second picture *(flowers)* may have selected it because flowers are a familiar gift for a mother.

Children who chose the third picture *(gift)* may not distinguish between a gift and a card.

36. **Correct response:** *country*

The correct answer is the vocabulary word *country*. If children write another word, such as *national* or *government,* they understand the concept and intent of the question but are not using a word they have learned. If children write a word that does not make sense as an answer to the question, they may not understand some of the words in the definition.

37. **Correct response:** *create*

The correct answer is the vocabulary word *create*. If children write another word, such as *put together* or *build,* they understand the concept and intent of the question but are not using a word they have learned. Children might respond with a word for something made, such as *card.* If so, point out that the needed word is for the action, not the product. If children write a word that does not make sense as an answer to the question, they may not understand some of the words in the definition.

(Vocabulary continued)

38. **Correct response:** *value*

    The correct answer is the vocabulary word *value*. If children write another word, such as *amount* or *dollars,* they understand the concept and intent of the question but are not using a word they have learned. If children name something that is purchased with money, emphasize that the word is a vocabulary word related to money's worth. If children write a word that does not make sense as an answer to the question, they may not understand some of the words in the definition.

39. **Correct response:** *neighbors*

    The correct answer is the vocabulary word *neighbors*. If children write other words, such as *friends* or *people next door,* they understand the concept and intent of the question but are not using a word they have learned. If children name specific people, remind them that they should give a vocabulary word that can be used for all people who live nearby. If children write a word that does not make sense as an answer to the question, they may not understand some of the words in the definition.

40. **Correct response:** *president*

    The correct answer is the vocabulary word *president*. If children write other words, such as *leader* or *head of state,* they understand the concept and intent of the question but are not using a word they have learned. If children name specific leaders, remind them that they should give a vocabulary word that can name leaders in general. If children write a word that does not make sense as an answer to the question, they may not understand some of the words in the definition.

Suggested Remediation: Review lesson vocabulary words by defining the terms and having children take turns using the words in sentences.

WRITING (Recommended Time: 15–20 minutes, uninterrupted)

Teacher Directions: Have children turn to page 22. Make sure they have pencils. Read the prompt aloud and point out the illustration on page 23. Make sure children know to draw their picture on page 24 and write their response on page 25. Then read through the writing checklist on page 27. You may wish to give children scrap paper to use to plan their writing, or permit them to use page 26 as scrap paper.

For the last part of the test, you will draw a picture and write at least two sentences about a topic I'm about to read to you. The topic explains what you are going to draw and write about. The topic also gives you some ideas for planning.

If you do not know how to spell a word, sound out the word and do the best you can. Write as neatly as you can. Be sure your sentences are about the topic. Here is the topic you should draw and write about:

(Writing continued)

Prompt:

In "Happy Birthday, America!" Felix, his family, and his neighbors celebrated our country's birthday. Think of a special celebration you have shared. What did you do? How did you help? Draw a picture of what happened. Then tell what happened in at least two complete sentences.

Point out the picture of the Fourth of July parade from "Happy Birthday, America!" Read the caption: **Here is Felix celebrating the Fourth of July with his family and neighbors.** Point out the drawing box on page 24 and the lines on page 25 for writing.

Then point out the checklist on page 27. Read the following to children.

Here are some things to remember when you are writing:

Did you draw the celebration you had?
Did you think about a special celebration you have shared?
Did you tell about what you did and how you helped?
Do your sentences make sense?
Do your sentences begin with a capital letter?
Do your sentences end with a punctuation mark?
Remember to look at your drawing.
Remember to write at least two complete sentences.
Remember to reread your sentences.

Now, think about what you would like to draw and write. You have 20 minutes. Remember to ask yourself the questions on page 27 after you are finished working. Make sure you have at least two complete sentences.

Be sure to answer any questions children may have. Read the prompt a second time. Alert them when they have five minutes remaining.

Scoring: See page xi of this manual for information on using how to score Writing.

5-Point Scoring Rubric

5	4	3	2	1
• writing is well focused on topic	• writing focused on topic	• writing generally focused on topic	• writing strays from topic	• writing is not focused on topic
• contains clear ideas	• most ideas are clear	• ideas are generally clear	• many ideas are unclear	• ideas are unclear
• demonstrates varied, precise word choice	• generally demonstrates varied, precise word choice	• word choice could be more varied, precise	• choice of words limited	• choice of words very limited
• sentences are complete	• most sentences are complete	• many sentences are complete	• many sentences are incomplete	• incomplete sentences
• shows excellent control of writing conventions	• shows very good control of writing conventions	• shows fairly good control of writing conventions	• shows frequent errors in writing conventions	• shows many serious errors in writing conventions

(Writing continued)

Sample Responses:

Possible student response (5-point score):

The whole family came to our house for Thanksgiving. We had a big dinner.

Possible student response (4-point score):

We went to a parade for community day. Lots of fun.

Possible student response (3-point score):

We play games. It is fun.

Possible student response (2-point score):

Go to fair Go on rides.

Possible student response (1-point score):

party balloons

FLUENCY (Time: 5–10 minutes preparation; 1 minute per student for reading)

Teacher Directions: Please refer to the "General Directions for the Administration of the Oral Reading Fluency Assessment" in this Teacher's Manual. Make enough copies of the following pages for each student. Do not provide students with a copy until test time.

Name ______________________________ Date ______________

Unit 4 Fluency

Teacher Copy

Say these specific directions to the student:
When I say "Begin," start reading aloud at the top of this page. Read across the page (DEMONSTRATE BY POINTING). *Try to read each word. If you come to a word you don't know, I will say the word for you. Read as quickly and accurately as you can, but do not read SO fast that you make mistakes. Do your best reading.*

The Camping Trip

Sam had an idea. He called Max. 7
"Let's camp out in my yard." 13

Sam and Max did not have a plan. 21
It was dark in the yard. 27
They did not have a flashlight. 33
Bugs buzzed around their arms and legs. 40
They did not have bug spray. 46

At last, Sam got the tent up. 53
Max set up two sleeping bags. 59
Sam saw a light in the dark. 66
Max saw something move. 70

Max and Sam were afraid. 75
They saw a dark shape crawl out from behind a bush. 86
"Can I join your campout?" asked Sam's little brother. 95

EVALUATING CODES FOR ORAL READING

~~sky~~	(/)	word read incorrectly
blue ^ sky	(^)	inserted word
	(])	after the last word read

Comments:

FLUENCY SCORE

Number of Words Read per Minute: ________

Number of Errors ________

Number of Words Read Correctly: ________

Errors include: 1) words read incorrectly; 2) words left out or inserted; 3) mispronounced words; 4) dropped endings or sounds; and 5) reversals. Self corrections and word repetitions are NOT marked as errors.

Name ______________________________ Date ______________

The Camping Trip

Sam had an idea. He called Max.

"Let's camp out in my yard."

Sam and Max did not have a plan.

It was dark in the yard.

They did not have a flashlight.

Bugs buzzed around their arms and legs.

They did not have bug spray.

At last, Sam got the tent up.

Max set up two sleeping bags.

Sam saw a light in the dark.

Max saw something move.

Max and Sam were afraid.

They saw a dark shape crawl out from behind a bush.

"Can I join your campout?" asked Sam's little brother.

Unit 4 Test Evaluation Chart

Name ______________________________ Date ________________

Item	Skill	Week/Day	Item/Type*	Assistance (circle)	Score (circle one)
1	Details and Facts	Week 3/4 Day 3	MC	Y N	0 1 2
2	Details and Facts	Week 3/4 Day 3	MC	Y N	0 1 2
3	Literary Elements: Setting	Week 5 Day 3	MC	Y N	0 1 2
4	Details and Facts	Week 3/4 Day 3	MC	Y N	0 1 2
5	Sequence	Week 5 Day 3	MC	Y N	0 1 2
6	Draw Conclusions	Week 1/2 Day 3	MC	Y N	0 1 2
7	Details and Facts	Week 3/4 Day 3	MC	Y N	0 1 2
8	Details and Facts	Week 3/4 Day 3	MC	Y N	0 1 2
9	Details and Facts	Week 3/4 Day 3	MC	Y N	0 1 2
10	Draw Conclusions	Week 1/2 Day 3	MC	Y N	0 1 2
11	Describing	Week 4 Day 3	MC	Y N	0 1 2
12	Past Tense Verbs	Week 5 Day 3	MC	Y N	0 1 2
13	Describing	Week 4 Day 3	MC	Y N	0 1 2
14	Past Tense Verbs	Week 5 Day 3	MC	Y N	0 1 2
15	Past Tense Verbs	Week 5 Day 3	MC	Y N	0 1 2
16	Adjectives	Week 2 Day 4	CR	Y N	0 1 2
17	Adjectives	Week 3 Day 4	CR	Y N	0 1 2
18	Adjectives	Week 3 Day 4	CR	Y N	0 1 2
19	Adjectives	Week 6 Day 4	CR	Y N	0 1 2
20	Adjectives	Week 6 Day 4	CR	Y N	0 1 2
21	Long *a* spelled *ai*	Week 6 Day 4	MC	Y N	0 1 2
22	Long *e* spelled *ea*	Week 1 Day 2	MC	Y N	0 1 2
23	Long *o* spelled *oa*	Week 2 Day 2	MC	Y N	0 1 2
24	Compound Words	Week 5 Day 2	MC	Y N	0 1 2
25	Compound Words	Week 5 Day 2	MC	Y N	0 1 2
26	Long *oo* spelled *oo*	Week 3 Day 2	CR	Y N	0 1 2
27	Long *u* spelled *ui*	Week 1 Day 2	CR	Y N	0 1 2
28	Long *e* spelled *ea*	Week 2 Day 2	CR	Y N	0 1 2
29	/n/ spelled *kn*	Week 3 Day 2	CR	Y N	0 1 2
30	/r/ spelled *wr*	Week 4 Day 2	CR	Y N	0 1 2
31	Vocabulary	Week 1 Day 1	MC	Y N	0 1 2
32	Vocabulary	Week 6 Day 1	MC	Y N	0 1 2
33	Vocabulary	Week 1 Day 1	MC	Y N	0 1 2
34	Vocabulary	Week 3 Day 1	MC	Y N	0 1 2
35	Vocabulary	Week 2 Day 1	MC	Y N	0 1 2
36	Vocabulary	Week 3 Day 1	CR	Y N	0 1 2
37	Vocabulary	Week 2 Day 1	CR	Y N	0 1 2
38	Vocabulary	Week 1 Day 1	CR	Y N	0 1 2
39	Vocabulary	Week 6 Day 1	CR	Y N	0 1 2
40	Vocabulary	Week 3 Day 1	CR	Y N	0 1 2
SCORE A: Skills and Content					____ out of 80
SCORE B: Writing				Y N	2 4 6 8 10
SCORE C: Fluency				WCPM ______	2 4 6 8 10
OVERALL SCORE					____ out of 100

*MC = multiple choice CR = constructed response

Grade 1, Unit 5
Answer Key and Directions

COMPREHENSION (Recommended Time: 30–45 minutes, uninterrupted)

Teacher Directions: Directions in **bold** are to be read aloud; others are for your information only. Use the following directions to administer the assessment. Make sure all children have a test booklet copy and pencils, and that children are on page 2 of the booklet. Explain that they will listen to a story and then answer some questions about it. Have students look at the picture and follow along as you read. Be sure to pause after each question so that children have time to mark their answers.

Read the following to the children:

Now I'm going to read a story about two men named Orville and Wilbur Wright and their invention. After the first part of the story, I will ask you some questions. Listen carefully. The story is called "An Invention That Changed the World." Here is the first part of the story.

An Invention That Changed the World

1 **Can you imagine a time before computers, television, or telephones?**
2 **What would your life be like without these amazing inventions?**
3 **Computers help us talk to people all over the world.**
4 **Television helps us learn things and have fun.**
5 **Airplanes changed the way we travel forever.**

Tell children to look at the next page.

6 **Before airplanes, people could not travel long distances easily.**
7 **They used wagons on land and boats on the sea.**
8 **It could take many days or weeks to go from one place to another.**

Tell children to turn to page 4.

9 **Orville Wright and his brother Wilbur made the first airplane.**
10 **Their first flight was over 100 years ago.**
11 **The flight lasted only a few seconds.**
12 **But their invention would soon change the world!**

Now model how to fill in the circle. Demonstrate the directions to the children, using a student test book. Read each question twice.

Now look at page 5. I am going to ask you some questions about this part of the story. For each question that I ask, you will see three pictures in a row. Ask yourself which picture goes with the question I ask. Fill in the circle below the picture that shows the best answer. Listen carefully.

(Comprehension continued)

1. **Look at the first row of pictures at the top of the page. What invention did the Wright brothers make? Was it *the computer . . . the airplane* . . . or *the car?* Put your finger on the picture that shows the invention that this story is about. Then fill in the circle below the picture you choose.**

2. **Point to the next row of pictures. How did people travel across the ocean before the airplane was invented? Did people travel by *boat . . . airplane* . . . or *helicopter?* Fill in the circle below the picture that shows the best answer.**

3. **Move down to the next row of pictures. How did people travel on land before the airplane was invented? Did people travel by *airplane . . . wagon* . . . or *boat?* Fill in the circle below the picture that shows the best answer.**

Ask children to turn to page 6.

4. **Look at the top row of pictures. What invention helps us talk to people all over the world? Is the invention *the car . . . the refrigerator* . . . or *the computer?* Fill in the circle below the picture that shows the best answer.**

5. **Look at the next row of pictures. Who invented the airplane? Were the inventors *two men . . . two women* . . . or *a boy and a girl?* Fill in the circle below the picture that shows the best answer.**

Look at page 7. Now I am going to read the second part of the story. Then I will ask you some more questions. Listen carefully. Here is the rest of the story.

An Invention That Changed the World (part 2)

Orville and Wilbur Wright sold bicycles. before they were inventors. They read books and watched birds fly. They worked hard for many years. The first airplane was named *Flyer*.

Now turn to page 8.

The Wright Brothers' invention changed how people travel. Long ago, it could take many days or weeks to cross the ocean. Today, an airplane ride across the ocean takes only hours. Maybe someday you will invent something that will change lives, just like the Wright Brothers!

Now the story about the inventors of the airplane is over, and I will ask you more questions. Look at page 9.

6. **Look at the first row of pictures. What did Orville and Wilbur Wright sell before they made airplanes? Did the brothers sell *bicycles . . . puzzles* . . . or *hats?* Put your finger on the picture that shows what the Wright Brothers sold. Then fill in the circle below that picture.**

(Comprehension continued)

7. **Move down to the next row of pictures. What animal did the Wright Brothers watch to learn about flying? Did the brothers watch *pigs . . . birds . . .* or *monkeys?* Fill in the circle below the picture that shows what the brothers watched to learn about flying.**
8. **Point to the next row of pictures. How is a bird like an airplane? Are birds like airplanes because they *have nests in trees . . . have wings . . .* or *peck at the ground?* Fill in the circle below the picture you choose.**

Ask children to turn to page 10.

9. **Why was *Flyer* a good name for the Wright Brothers' invention? Is it because *it was a bicycle . . . it was an airplane . . .* or *it was a boat?* Fill in the circle next to the sentence that you choose.**
10. **Which invention would you use to travel across the ocean fast? Is it *a car . . . a ship . . .* or *an airplane?* Fill in the circle next to your answer.**

<u>**Scoring:**</u> Photocopy and use the evaluation chart to track student scores and progress.

<u>**Comprehension Answer Key with Interpretation:**</u>

1. What invention did the Wright Brothers make?

Children who chose the first picture (computer) may have selected it because computers are amazing inventions also mentioned in the article.

Correct answer: second picture (airplane)

Children who chose the third picture (car) may have selected it because a car is a way to travel.

(Comprehension continued)

2. How did people travel across the ocean before the airplane was invented?

Correct answer: first picture (boat)

Children who chose the second picture (airplane) may have selected it because the airplane is the main topic of the passage.

Children who chose the third picture (helicopter) may not have distinguished between a helicopter and an airplane, which is the main topic of the article.

3. How did people travel on land before the airplane was invented?

Children who chose the first picture (airplane) may have selected it because they did not know the meaning of the word *before.*

Correct answer: second picture (wagon)

Children who chose the third picture (boat) may not have focused on the phrase "on land."

4. What invention helps us talk to people all over the world?

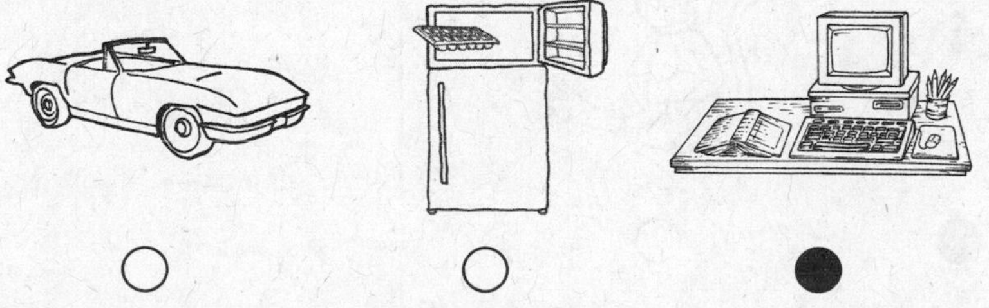

Children who chose the first picture (car) may have thought the question is asking about travel all over the world.

Children who chose the second picture (refrigerator) may not have understood the question.

Correct answer: third picture (computer)

(Comprehension continued)

5. Who invented the airplane?

Correct answer: first picture (two men)

Children who chose the second picture (two women) may not have understood the meaning of the word *brothers.*

Children who chose the third picture (a boy and a girl) did not connect text with picture clues.

6. What did Orville and Wilbur Wright sell before they made airplanes?

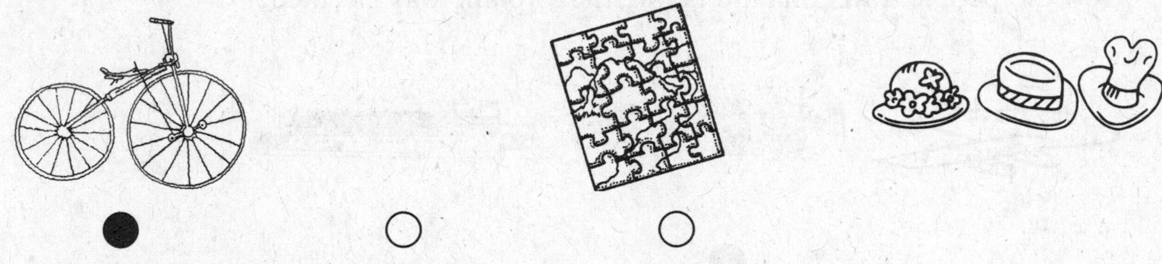

Correct answer: first picture (bicycle)

Children who chose the second picture (a puzzle) may not have understood how the word *puzzle* is used in the passage.

Children who chose the third picture (hats) may have selected it because they saw hats in another illustration.

7. What animal did the Wright Brothers watch to learn about flying?

Children who chose the first picture (pig) may have selected the first animal shown.

Correct answer: second picture (bird)

Children who chose the third picture (monkey) may have selected it because the monkey is up in a tree.

(Comprehension continued)

8. How is a bird like an airplane?

Children who chose the first picture (bird with baby birds) may have selected it because it shows a bird high off the ground.

Correct answer: second picture (bird with wings in motion)

Children who chose the third picture (bird on ground) may have selected it because they did not understand the question.

9. Why was *Flyer* a good name for the Wright Brothers' invention?

Children who chose the first sentence (It was a bicycle.) may have selected it because the Wright Brothers sold bicycles.

Correct answer: second sentence (It was an airplane.)

Children who chose the third sentence (It was a boat.) might have selected it because they did not understand the passage.

10. Which invention would you use to travel across the ocean fast?

Children who chose the first answer (a car) may have selected it because they are most familiar with a car as a means of transportation.

Children who chose the second answer (a ship) may have selected it because ships do cross the ocean.

Correct answer: third answer (an airplane)

<u>**Suggested Remediation:**</u> Discuss each part of the reading selection, using the pictures and words to identify the main idea and details and to make comparisons and contrasts. Reread the selection with students and model how to draw conclusions.

CHECKING SKILLS (Recommended Time: 20 minutes, uninterrupted)

<u>**Teacher Directions:**</u> Use the following directions to administer the assessment. Read the sentences aloud more than once if needed. Be sure to pause after each question so that children have time to mark their answers. Make sure all children are on page 11 before you begin.

(Checking Skills continued)

Read the following directions to children:

Now I am going to read some sentences to you. The sentences I will read tell about people and travel. Pick the picture that goes with the sentence that I read. Listen carefully.

11. Look at the pictures at the top of the page. Here is the sentence: *The airplane flies over the town.* Which picture shows an airplane flying over a town? Point to that picture. Fill in the circle below the picture you choose.

12. Put your finger next to the second row of pictures. Look at those three pictures. Here is the sentence: *The tree is taller than the girl.* Find the picture that shows a tree that is taller than a girl. Fill in the circle below that picture.

13. Look at the next row of pictures. Here is the sentence: *They fly the airplane.* Find the picture that shows people flying an airplane. Point to that picture. Fill in the circle below the picture.

Now turn to page 12.

14. Put your finger next to the top row of pictures. Here is the sentence: *His brother flew the airplane over him.* Which picture shows an airplane flown over one person? Fill in the circle below that picture.

15. Now look at the last row of pictures on the page. Here is the sentence: *First, he packs a backpack.* Which picture shows someone packing a backpack? Fill in the circle below that picture.

Look at page 13. Now I will read a sentence for each picture you see. Follow along in your book while I read aloud. Then you will add the end punctuation to the sentence.

16. Do you see the airplane
Add the punctuation mark that makes this a question.

17. Look at that
Add the punctuation mark that makes this an exclamation.

18. May I sit by the window
Add the punctuation mark that makes this a question.

Now turn to page 14.

19. Pack your suitcase
Add the punctuation mark that makes this a command.

20. The airplane is loud
Add the punctuation mark that makes this an exclamation.

Scoring: Photocopy and use the evaluation chart to track student scores and progress.

(Checking Skills continued)

11. The airplane flies **over** the town.

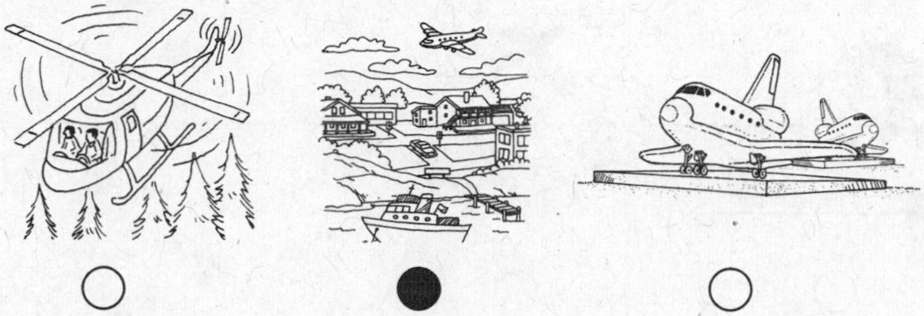

Children who chose the first picture (helicopter over trees) may not have distinguished between an airplane and a helicopter or paid attention to where the airplane was flying.

Correct answer: second picture (airplane flying over town)

Children who chose the third picture (an airplane on the ground) may not have distinguished position words.

12. The tree is **taller** than the girl.

Children who chose the first picture (two flowers) may not have understood that the sentence compares different objects of different sizes.

Children who chose the second picture (two trees of different sizes) may not have related text to pictured items.

Correct answer: third picture (girl standing near tree)

13. **They** fly the airplane.

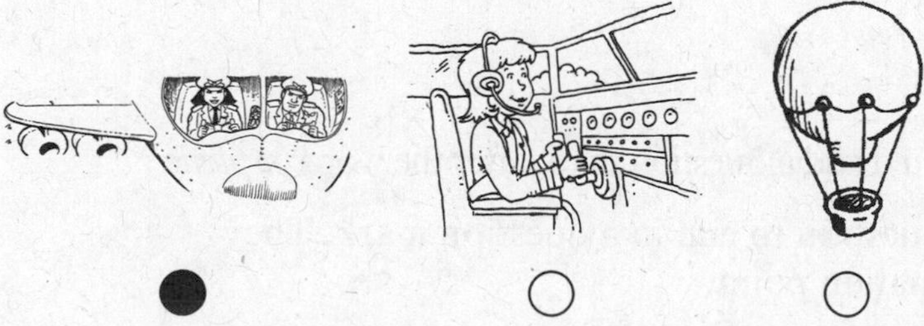

Correct answer: first picture (two people flying an airplane)

Children who chose the second picture (one person flying an airplane) may not have differentiated singular and plural pronouns.

Children who chose the third picture (hot-air balloon) may not have distinguished between a hot-air balloon and an airplane.

(Checking Skills continued)

14. His brother flew the airplane over **him.**

Correct answer: first picture (airplane flying over a man)

Children who chose the second picture (child making a model airplane) may not have related text to pictured items.

Children who chose the third picture (airplane flying over a group of people) may not have differentiated singular and plural pronouns.

15. **First,** he packs a backpack.

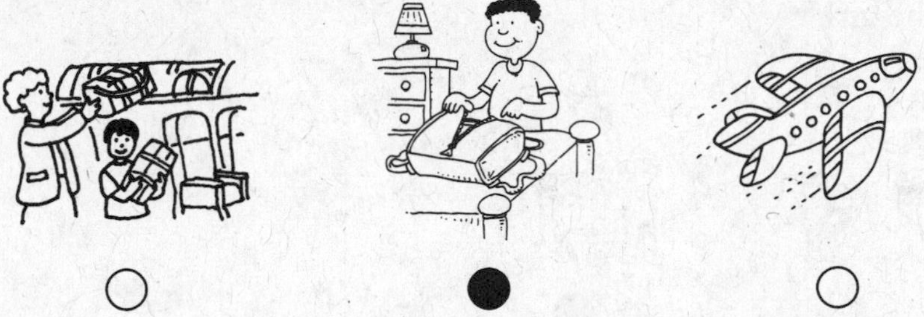

Children who chose the first picture (two people putting a suitcase in an overhead bin) may not have understood words that indicate sequence.

Correct answer: second picture (person packing a backpack)

Children who chose the third picture (an airplane flying away) may not have understood the sequence of events.

Suggested Remediation: Have students take turns giving clues about objects in the classroom using prepositions that tell location and comparative adjectives.

16. Do you see the airplane

Correct response: Children should add a question mark after the word *airplane.*

Children may not identify a question to end in a question mark. They may use a period or an exclamation point.

17. Look at that

Correct response: Children should add an exclamation point after the word *that.*

Children may not identify an exclamation to end in an exclamation point. They may use a period or question mark.

(**Checking Skills continued**)

18. May I sit by the window

    Correct response: Children should add a question mark after the word *window.*

    Children may not identify a question to end in a question mark. They may use a period or an exclamation point.

19. Pack your suitcase

    Correct response: Children should add a period after the word *suitcase.*

    Children may not identify a command to end in a period. They may use a question mark or an exclamation point.

20. The airplane is loud

    Correct response: Children should add an exclamation point after the word *loud.*

    Children may not identify an exclamation to end in an exclamation point. They may use a period or question mark.

Suggested Remediation: Write a period, question mark, and exclamation point on the board. Model the four different sentence types and point to the corresponding end marks on the board. Then have students form declarative, interrogative, imperative, and exclamatory sentences and choose the correct end marks.

WORD ANALYSIS (Recommended Time: 20–30 minutes, uninterrupted)

Teacher Directions: Have the children turn to page 15. Use the following directions to administer the assessment. Read the words and sentences aloud more than once if needed. Be sure to pause after each question so that children have time to mark their answers.

Read the following directions to children:

Now we are going to match the pictures to the words on the page. Listen carefully. You will decide which word goes with the picture.

21. Put your finger on the picture at the top of the page. What do you see in the picture? Next look at the three words. Does that picture show *a crow* . . . *a cow* . . . or *a car?* Fill in the circle below the word you choose.

22. Look at the second picture. Does that picture show *a mouse* . . . *a mask* . . . or *mow?* Fill in the circle below the word you choose.

23. Point to the third picture. What does it show? Does the picture show *hike* . . . *a hook* . . . or *a hat?* Fill in the circle below the word you choose.

(Word Analysis continued)

Turn to page 16.

24. Put your finger on the picture at the top of the page. What do you see in the picture? Next look at the three words. The words are *renew . . . repack . . .* and *reread.* Fill in the circle next to the word you choose.

25. Look at the second picture. What does the picture show? The words are *unwrap . . . unhappy . . .* and *unstuck.* Fill in the circle next to the word you choose.

Look at page 17. Now we will study words. This time you will decide what vowel sound a word makes. Then you will write a word that makes the same vowel sound.

26. Look at the picture at the top of the page. The picture shows a bear. The word is *bear*. Write a word that has the same vowel sound as the word *bear*.

27. Look at the next picture. The picture shows a coin. The word is *coin.* Write a word that has the same vowel sound as the word *coin.*

28. Move on to the next picture. The picture shows a cloud. The word is *cloud.* Write a word that has the same vowel sound as the word *cloud.*

Now turn to page 18.

29. Look at the picture at the top of the page. The picture shows a boy. The word is *boy*. Write a word that has the same vowel sound as the word *boy*.

30. Look at the next picture. The picture shows straw. The word is *straw*. Write a word that has the same vowel sound as the word *straw*.

<u>Scoring</u>: Photocopy and use the evaluation chart to track children's scores and progress.

<u>Word Analysis Answer Key with Interpretation:</u>

21. Children who chose the first word (crow) did not distinguish long *o* from /ou/.

Correct answer: *cow*

Children who chose the third word (car) did not distinguish /ar/ from /ou/.

22. **Correct answer:** *mouse*

Children who chose the second word (mask) did not distinguish short *a* from /ou/ or the ending sound.

Children who chose the third word (mow) did not distinguish long *o* from /ou/.

23. Children who chose the first word (hike) did not distinguish long *i* from /ü/.

Correct answer: *hook*

Children who chose the third word (hat) did not distinguish short *a* from /ü/.

(Word Analysis continued)

Suggested Remediation: Place a large card with each vowel pattern on the wall. Distribute word cards with corresponding vowel patterns to children. Have them place the word cards under the corresponding vowel pattern. Have children read the words aloud.

24. Children who chose the first word (renew) may not know the meaning of the root word *new.*

    Correct answer: *repack*

    Children who chose the third word (reread) may not know the meaning of the root word *read.*

25. **Correct answer:** *unwrap*

    Children who chose the second word (unhappy) may not know the meaning of the root word *happy.*

    Children who chose the third word (unstuck) may not know the meaning of the root word *stuck.*

Suggested Remediation: Have children pantomime the words *tie, retie,* and *untie* to demonstrate the meaning of the prefixes *re-* and *un-*.

26. **Possible answers:** *pear, fair*

    Children who gave other responses such as *beet* or *fur* may have chosen words with the same beginning or ending sounds.

27. **Possible answers:** *boil, soil, join, noise*

    Children who gave other responses such as *can* and *mean* may have chosen words with the same beginning or ending sounds.

28. **Possible answers:** *house, round, count, mouth*

    Children who gave other responses such as *cut* or *hot* did not distinguish /ou/ from short vowel *o* and *u.*

29. **Possible answers:** *toy, joy*

    Children who gave other responses such as *show* or *coat* did not distinguish /oi/ from long *o* patterns.

30. **Possible answers:** *law, claw, draw, saw, jaw*

    Children who gave other responses such as *stripe* or *straight* may have chosen words with the same beginning sounds.

Suggested Remediation: Say a series of words and ask children to choose the word that does not have the same vowel sound as the others. Use these words: *mouth, sprout, moon; pear, bear, plow; cook, stood, cool; joy, toy, took; park, saw, paw.*

VOCABULARY (Recommended Time: 20–30 minutes, uninterrupted)

Teacher Directions: Have the children turn to page 19. Use the following directions to administer the assessment.

Read the following directions to children:
Now we will choose pictures that match sentences.

31. **Read the sentence *The bee flew to the flower.* Look at the three pictures. Which picture shows the sentence *The bee flew to the flower?* Fill in the circle below the picture you choose.**

32. **Read the sentence *Pam was upside down on the beam.* Look at the three pictures. Which picture shows the sentence *Pam was upside down on the beam?* Fill in the circle below the picture you choose.**

33. **Read the sentence *The boy pulled the fish out of the water.* Look at the three pictures. Which picture shows the sentence *The boy pulled the fish out of the water?* Fill in the circle below the picture you choose.**

Turn to page 20.

34. **Read the sentence *The closet was full of clothes.* Look at the three pictures. Which picture shows the sentence *The closet was full of clothes?* Fill in the circle below the picture you choose.**

35. **Read the sentence *Bill bent down to retie his shoe.* Look at the three pictures. Which picture shows in the sentence *Bill bent down to retie his shoe?* Fill in the circle below the picture you choose.**

Look at page 21. Now I will read you questions. You will write the answer. Your answer can be one word. Write the word on the line. Listen carefully.

Be sure to read the questions slowly and, if needed, more than once.

36. **Look at the picture at the top of the page. What do you call the letters and packages that are delivered to a place? Write that word on the line.**

37. **Put your finger on the next picture. What do you do when you make something by putting pieces together? Write that word on the line.**

38. **Look at the next picture. What is a thought or a plan that you think of? Write the word on the line.**

39. **Move down to the next picture. What do you call a vehicle with four wheels that is usually pulled by horses? Write the word on the line.**

40. The last question does not have a picture as a clue. **Listen carefully. What do you call things that help you find the answer to a difficult problem? Write the word on the line.**

Scoring: Photocopy and use the evaluation chart to track student scores and progress.

(Vocabulary continued)

Vocabulary Answer Key with Interpretation:

31. The bee **flew** to the flower.

Correct response: first picture (bee on flower)

Children who chose the second picture (hummingbird on flower) did not distinguish between a bee and a hummingbird.

Children who chose the third picture (airplane) may have selected it because an airplane flies.

32. Pam was **upside down** on the beam.

Children who chose the first picture (girl standing on beam) may not have understood position words.

Correct answer: second picture (girl doing handstand)

Children who chose the third picture (girl next to a beam) may not have understood position words.

33. The boy **pulled** the fish out of the water.

Children who chose the first picture (fish in fishbowl) may have selected it because they did not listen to the entire sentence.

Children who chose the second picture (person swimming) may have selected it because it shows someone in the water.

Correct answer: third picture (boys fishing)

(Vocabulary continued)

34. The **closet** was full of clothes.

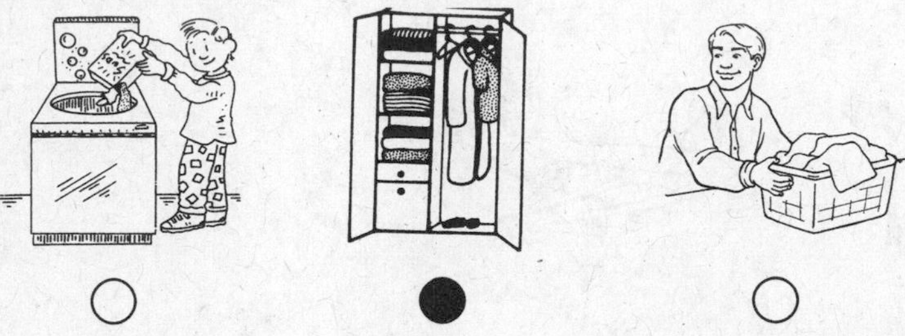

Children who chose the first picture (washing machine) may have selected it because clothes can be found in a washing machine.

Correct answer: second picture (clothes in closet)

Children who chose the third picture (person with laundry) may have selected it because it shows clothes.

35. Bill bent down to **retie** his shoe.

Children who chose the first picture (boy tying a bow) may have selected it because they do not understand the meaning of the prefix *re-*.

Children who chose the second picture (boy putting on a coat) may have selected it because they did not understand the sentence.

Correct answer: third picture (boy tying shoe)

36. **Correct response:** *mail*

The correct answer is the vocabulary word *mail.* If children write another word, such as *letters* or *deliveries,* they understand the concept and intent of the question but are not using a word they have learned. If children write a word that does not make sense as an answer to the question, they may not understand some of the words in the definition.

37. **Correct response:** *build*

The correct answer is the vocabulary word *build.* If children write other words, such as *put together, make,* or *construct,* they understand the concept and intent of the question but are not using a word they have learned. Children might respond with a word for something made, such as *puzzle* or *house.* If so, point out that the correct word is for the action, not for what is being made.

(**Vocabulary continued**)

38. **Correct response:** *idea*

    The correct answer is the vocabulary word *idea.* If children write another word, such as *thought,* they understand the concept and intent of the question but are not using a word they have learned. If children name a specific idea, help them understand that you are looking for a word that will name all thoughts and plans, not just one. If children write a word that does not make sense as an answer to the question, they may not understand some of the words in the definition.

39. **Correct response:** *wagon*

    The correct answer is the vocabulary word *wagon.* If children write another word, such as *carriage* or *cart,* they understand the concept and intent of the question but are not using a word they have learned. If children name something related to horses such as *riding* or *saddle,* remind them that the word is for something that horses pull.

40. **Correct response:** *clues*

    The correct answer is the vocabulary word *clues.* If children write another word, such as *hints,* they understand the concept and intent of the question but are not using a word they have learned. If children write a word that does not make sense as an answer to the question, they may not understand some of the words in the definition. You might give them examples of clues to help them identify the word.

Suggested Remediation: Review lesson vocabulary words by playing a matching game. Help children write definitions and vocabulary words on separate cards. Mix the cards and place them face up on a table. Have children take turns choosing a word card and matching it with a definition card.

WRITING (Recommended Time: 15–20 minutes, uninterrupted)

Teacher Directions: Have children turn to page 22. Make sure they have pencils. Read the prompt aloud and point out the illustration on page 23. Make sure children know to draw their picture on page 24 and write their response on page 25. Then read through the writing checklist on page 27. You may wish to give children scrap paper to use to plan their writing, or permit them to use page 26 as scrap paper.

Read the following directions to children:
For the last part of the test, you will write draw a picture and write three sentences about a topic I'm about to read to you. The topic explains what you are going to draw and write about. The topic also gives you some ideas for planning.

(Writing continued)

If you do not know how to spell a word, sound out the word and do the best you can. Write as neatly as you can. Be sure your sentences are about the topic. Here is the topic you should write about:

Prompt:

In "An Invention That Changed the World," the Wright Brothers invented the airplane to make travel easier. Think of an invention you use that makes your life easier. What is the invention? How do you use it? How does the invention make your life easier? Draw the invention. Then write three complete sentences.

Point out the picture of the Wright Brothers and their airplane on page 23. Read the caption: **The Wright Brothers' invention, the airplane, changed the world.** Point out the drawing box on page 24 and the lines on page 25 for writing.

Then point out the checklist on page 27. Read the following directions to children.

Here are some things to remember when you are writing:
Did you draw an invention?
Did you think about an invention that makes your life easier?
Did you tell how you use the invention?
Do sentences make sense?
Do your sentences begin with a capital letter?
Do your sentences end with a punctuation mark?
Remember to look at your drawing.
Remember to write three complete sentences.
Remember to reread your sentences.

Now, think about what you would like to draw and write. You have 20 minutes. Remember to ask yourself the questions on page 27 after you are finished working. Make sure you write three complete sentences.

Be sure to answer any questions children may have. Read the prompt a second time. Alert them when they have five minutes remaining.

(Writing continued)

Scoring: See page xi of this manual for information on how to score Writing.

5-Point Scoring Rubric

5	4	3	2	1
• writing is well focused on topic	• writing focused on topic	• writing generally focused on topic	• writing strays from topic	• writing is not focused on topic
• contains clear ideas	• most ideas are clear	• ideas are generally clear	• many ideas are unclear	• ideas are unclear
• demonstrates varied, precise word choice	• generally demonstrates varied, precise word choice	• word choice could be more varied, precise	• choice of words limited	• choice of words very limited
• sentences are complete	• most sentences are complete	• many sentences are complete	• many sentences are incomplete	• incomplete sentences
• shows excellent control of writing conventions	• shows very good control of writing conventions	• shows fairly good control of writing conventions	• shows frequent errors in writing conventions	• shows many serious errors in writing conventions

Sample Responses:

Possible response (5-point score):

I use a computer. It helps me learn to read and do math. I can play games on it too.

Possible response (4-point score):

The hair dryer blow my hair. My hair dries. Then I go outside.

Possible response (3-point score):

I use Mom phone. I call my ant we tak

Possible response (2-point score):

The TV is gud. Watch for fun

Possible response (1-point score):

i like muzc plaer.

FLUENCY (Time: 5–10 minutes preparation; 1 minute per student for reading)

Teacher Directions: Please refer to the "General Directions for the Administration of the Oral Reading Fluency Assessment" in this Teacher's Manual. Make enough copies of the following pages for each student. Do not provide students with a copy until test time.

Name ______________________________ Date ______________

Unit 5 Fluency

Teacher Copy

Say these specific directions to the student:
When I say "Begin," start reading aloud at the top of this page. Read across the page (DEMONSTRATE BY POINTING). *Try to read each word. If you come to a word you don't know, I will say the word for you. Read as quickly and accurately as you can, but do not read SO fast that you make mistakes. Do your best reading.*

All About Ducks

Ducks are birds that live in water.	7
They are good swimmers and fishers.	13
Some ducks have short wings.	18
Short wings help ducks dive for food.	25
Some ducks have long necks.	30
Long necks help ducks pick food out of the water.	40
Some ducks have wide bills.	45
They sift seeds and snails from the water.	53
Ducks have two webbed feet.	58
Their feet are like paddles.	63
Webbed feet help ducks swim and dive.	70
Ducks don't get wet.	74
They have a gland under their tail that makes oil.	84
Ducks rub oil on their feathers.	90
Water rolls off their feathers.	95
Ducks are waterproof birds!	99

EVALUATING CODES FOR ORAL READING

~~sky~~	(/)	word read incorrectly
blue ^ sky	(^)	inserted word
	(])	after the last word read

Comments:

FLUENCY SCORE

Number of Words Read per Minute: ________

Number of Errors ________

Number of Words Read Correctly: ________

Errors include: 1) words read incorrectly; 2) words left out or inserted; 3) mispronounced words; 4) dropped endings or sounds; and 5) reversals. Self corrections and word repetitions are NOT marked as errors.

Name ______________________________ Date ______________

Unit 5 Fluency **Student Copy**

All About Ducks

Ducks are birds that live in water.
They are good swimmers and fishers.
Some ducks have short wings.
Short wings help ducks dive for food.
Some ducks have long necks.
Long necks help ducks pick food out of the water.
Some ducks have wide bills.
They sift seeds and snails from the water.

Ducks have two webbed feet.
Their feet are like paddles.
Webbed feet help ducks swim and dive.

Ducks don't get wet.
They have a gland under their tail that makes oil.
Ducks rub oil on their feathers.
Water rolls off their feathers.
Ducks are waterproof birds!

Unit 5 Test Evaluation Chart

Name ______________________________ **Date** ______________

Item	Skill	Week/Day	Item/ Type*	Assistance (circle)	Score (circle one)
1	Main Idea and Details	Week 3 Day 3	MC	Y N	0 1 2
2	Main Idea and Details	Week 3 Day 3	MC	Y N	0 1 2
3	Main Idea and Details	Week 3 Day 3	MC	Y N	0 1 2
4	Main Idea and Details	Week 3 Day 3	MC	Y N	0 1 2
5	Main Idea and Details	Week 3 Day 3	MC	Y N	0 1 2
6	Sequence	Week 2 Day 3	MC	Y N	0 1 2
7	Main Idea and Details	Week 3 Day 3	MC	Y N	0 1 2
8	Compare and Contrast	Week 1/6 Day 3	MC	Y N	0 1 2
9	Draw Conclusions	Week 5 Day 3	MC	Y N	0 1 2
10	Draw Conclusions	Week 5 Day 3	MC	Y N	0 1 2
11	Describing	Week 4 Day 3	MC	Y N	0 1 2
12	Comparing	Week 6 Day 3	MC	Y N	0 1 2
13	Pronouns	Week 4 Day 4	MC	Y N	0 1 2
14	Pronouns	Week 4 Day 4	MC	Y N	0 1 2
15	Sequencing	Week 2 Day 2	MC	Y N	0 1 2
16	Interrogative Sentences/End Marks	Week 3 Day 4	CR	Y N	0 1 2
17	Exclamatory Sentences/End Marks	Week 2 Day 4	CR	Y N	0 1 2
18	Interrogative Sentences/End Marks	Week 3 Day 4	CR	Y N	0 1 2
19	Imperative Sentences/End Marks	Week 1 Day 4	CR	Y N	0 1 2
20	Exclamatory Sentences/End Marks	Week 2 Day 4	CR	Y N	0 1 2
21	*/ou/* spelled *ow*	Week 1 Day 2	MC	Y N	0 1 2
22	*/ou/* spelled *ou*	Week 2 Day 2	MC	Y N	0 1 2
23	Short *oo* spelled *oo*	Week 3 Day 2	MC	Y N	0 1 2
24	Prefix *re-*	Week 1 Day 2	MC	Y N	0 1 2
25	Prefix *un-*	Week 1 Day 2	MC	Y N	0 1 2
26	*/e/* spelled *ea*	Week 5 Day 2	CR	Y N	0 1 2
27	*/oi/* spelled *oi*	Week 4 Day 2	CR	Y N	0 1 2
28	*/ou/* spelled *ou*	Week 2 Day 2	CR	Y N	0 1 2
29	*/oi/* spelled *oy*	Week 4 Day 2	CR	Y N	0 1 2
30	*/ö/* spelled *aw*	Week 5 Day 2	CR	Y N	0 1 2
31	Vocabulary	Week 2 Day 1	MC	Y N	0 1 2
32	Vocabulary	Week 2 Day 1	MC	Y N	0 1 2
33	Vocabulary	Week 1 Day 1	MC	Y N	0 1 2
34	Vocabulary	Week 3 Day 1	MC	Y N	0 1 2
35	Vocabulary	Week 6 Day 1	MC	Y N	0 1 2
36	Vocabulary	Week 5 Day 1	CR	Y N	0 1 2
37	Vocabulary	Week 6 Day 1	CR	Y N	0 1 2
38	Vocabulary	Week 4 Day 1	CR	Y N	0 1 2
39	Vocabulary	Week 1 Day 1	CR	Y N	0 1 2
40	Vocabulary	Week 3 Day 1	CR	Y N	0 1 2
SCORE A: Skills and Content					____ **out of 80**
SCORE B: Writing Sentences				Y N	2 4 6 8 10
SCORE C: Fluency				WCPM ______	2 4 6 8 10
OVERALL SCORE					____ **out of 100**

***MC = multiple choice CR = constructed response**

NAME ______________________________ DATE ____________

Progress Monitoring Assessment

Readiness Unit Test

Homes and Families

Glenview, Illinois • Boston, Massachusetts • Chandler, Arizona • Upper Saddle River, New Jersey

1 2 3 4 5 6 7 8 9 10 V0N4 14 13 12 11 10

COMPREHENSION

DIRECTIONS: Read or listen to the story about Dan and Baby Sam.

Dan and Baby Sam

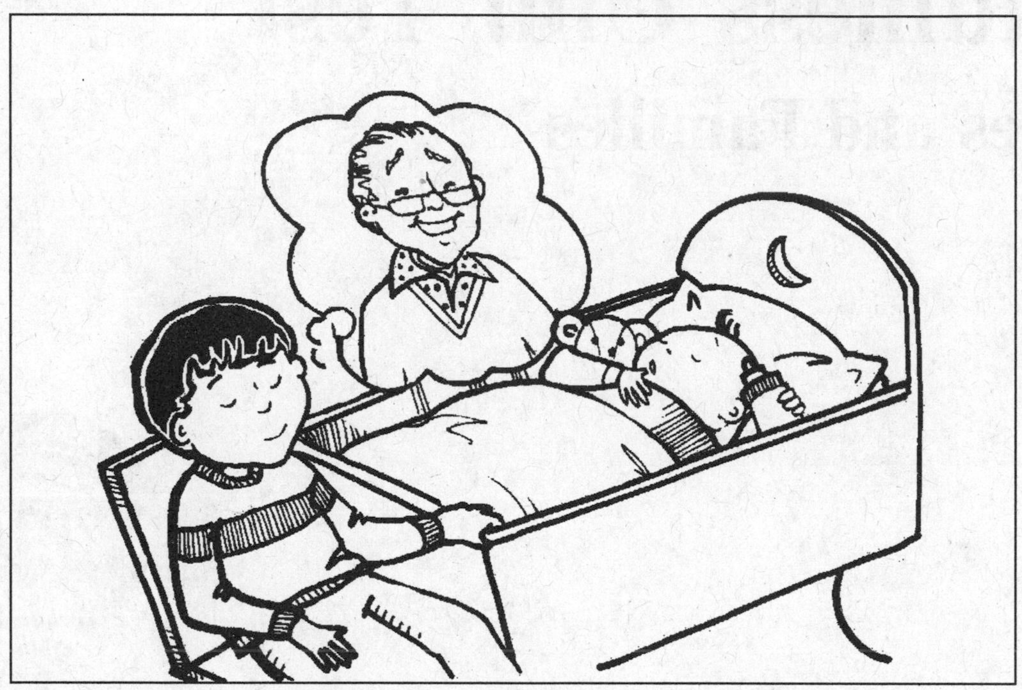

Today was the big day! Grandpa was coming to Dan's house. He wants to see Dan's new baby brother, Sam.

Dan was very happy. He hoped Grandpa would read him a story. He hoped they would play with Dan's trains.

Grandpa gave Dan a big hug. Then he went to see Baby Sam. Grandpa did not play with Dan. Dan was very sad.

Now answer the questions about this part of the story.

(Comprehension continued)

DIRECTIONS: Listen to your teacher. Choose the correct answer.

○ ○ ○

2

○  

3

○ ○ ○

(Comprehension continued)

DIRECTIONS: Listen to your teacher. Choose the correct answer.

5

(Comprehension continued)

Dan and Baby Sam (part 2)

11 Grandpa played with Baby Sam.

12 Dan sat in his room all alone.

13 Dan was very sad.

14 "Dan, what is wrong?" Grandpa asked.

"No one will play with me," said Dan. "Come with me," said Grandpa. Dan did. "I will read a story to you and Sam," Grandpa said. Dan liked to read with Grandpa and Sam.

Now answer the questions about this part of the story.

(Comprehension continued)

DIRECTIONS: Listen to your teacher. Choose the correct answer.

○ ○ ○

7

○ ○ ○

8

○ ○ ○

(Comprehension continued)

DIRECTIONS: Listen to your teacher. Choose the correct answer.

CHECKING SKILLS

DIRECTIONS: Listen to your teacher. Choose the correct answer.

12

13

(Checking Skills continued)

DIRECTIONS: Listen to your teacher. Choose the correct answer.

(Checking Skills continued)

DIRECTIONS: Listen to your teacher. Write the correct answer.

16 Dan sat in his room.

17 The baby smiled.

18 Grandpa played with Baby Sam.

(Checking Skills continued)

DIRECTIONS: Listen to your teacher. Write the correct answer.

19

Grandpa was coming to Dan's ____________________.

20

Dan was very ____________________.

WORD ANALYSIS

DIRECTIONS: Listen to your teacher. Choose the correct word.

21 vet ○ man ○ van ○

22 run ○ bun ○ ram ○

23 cap ○ cat ○ can ○

(Word Analysis continued)

DIRECTIONS: Listen to your teacher. Choose the correct sentence.

- ○ Dogs like dig.
- ○ The dog likes to dig.
- ○ The dog likes.

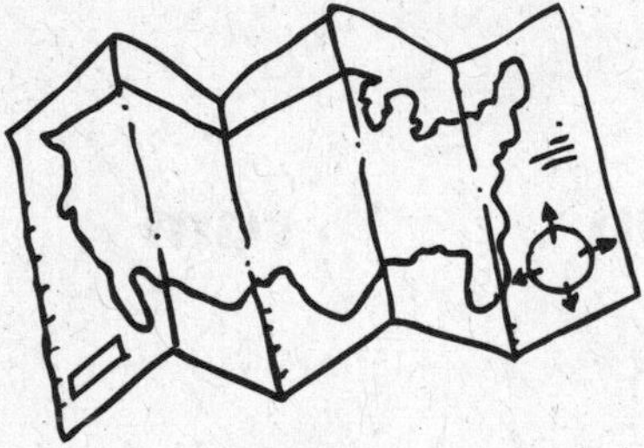

- ○ This is my map.
- ○ These maps me.
- ○ The map is four.

(Word Analysis continued)

DIRECTIONS: Listen to your teacher. Choose the word that has the same beginning letter sound.

26

- ○ **pan**
- ○ **fun**
- ○ **mat**

27

- ○ **sail**
- ○ **mitt**
- ○ **pats**

(Word Analysis continued)

DIRECTIONS: Listen to your teacher. Choose the word that has the same beginning letter sound.

28 ball ○ web ○ mat ○

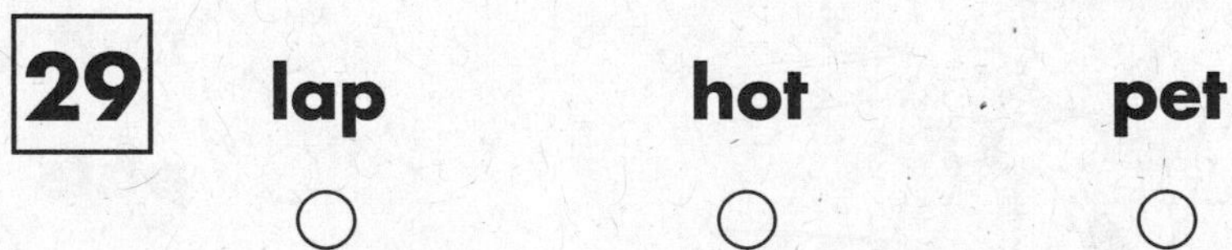

29 lap ○ hot ○ pet ○

30 pail ○ lap ○ real ○

VOCABULARY

DIRECTIONS: Listen to your teacher. Read the sentences. Choose the correct answer.

31 The children learn in a **classroom.**

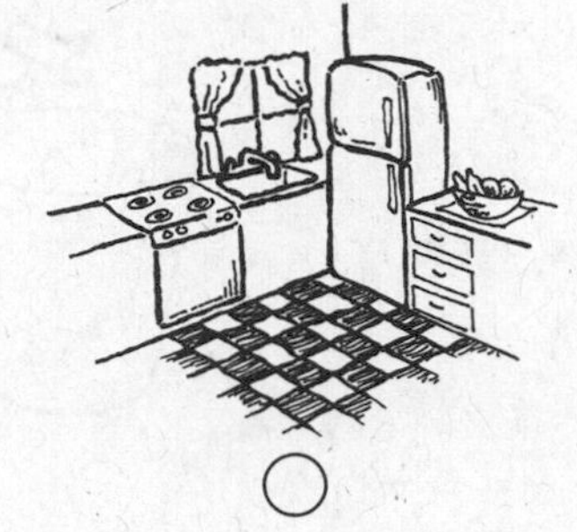

○ ○ ○

32 A **bird** can fly.

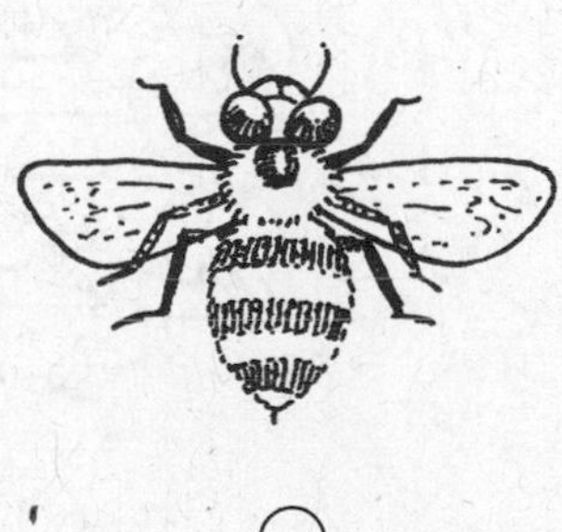

○ ○ ○

33 The **fruit** is sweet.

○ ○ ○

(Vocabulary continued)

DIRECTIONS: Listen to your teacher. Read the sentences. Choose the correct answer.

34 I carry a **backpack.**

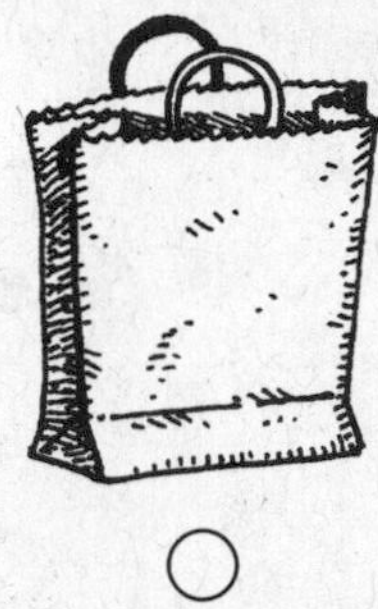

○ ○ ○

35 You can **buy** food.

○ ○ ○

(Vocabulary continued)

DIRECTIONS: Listen to your teacher. Write the correct word.

36

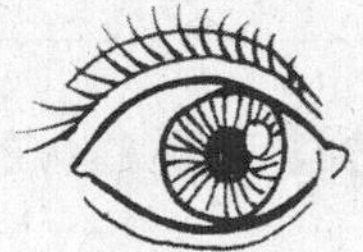

37

38

39

40

WRITING

DIRECTIONS: Listen to your teacher. Draw on page 24. Write on page 25. Use the checklist on page 27 for help.

PROMPT

In "Dan and Baby Sam," Dan is excited to play with his Grandpa.

Think of something you like to do with a member of your family.

- Who do you like to play with?
- What do you do?

Draw a picture of the family member and the activity. Then write 2 complete sentences.

Here is Dan reading with Grandpa.

Draw your picture here.

Write your sentences here.

THIS PAGE LEFT INTENTIONALLY BLANK

(Writing continued)

WRITING CHECKLIST

Put a ✓ check next to the things you did.

Did you:

- ☐ draw a picture of the family member and the activity?
- ☐ think about what you like to do with someone in your family?
- ☐ tell about what you like to do with that person?

Do your sentences:

- ☐ make sense?
- ☐ begin with a capital letter?
- ☐ end with a punctuation mark?

Remember to:

- ☐ look at your drawing.
- ☐ write two complete sentences.
- ☐ reread your sentences.

NAME ______________________ DATE ____________

Progress Monitoring Assessment

Unit 1 Test

Animals, Tame and Wild

Glenview, Illinois • Boston, Massachusetts • Chandler, Arizona • Upper Saddle River, New Jersey

1 2 3 4 5 6 7 8 9 10 V0N4 14 13 12 11 10

COMPREHENSION

DIRECTIONS: Read or listen to the story about Matt and his cat named Mittens.

Mittens

My name is Matt and I have a pet cat named Mittens. One day, Mittens looked sick. My mom and I left our apartment and took her to the vet.

I held Mittens with care and protected her.

We drove through the city.

When we got to the doctor, the vet examined Mittens and smiled. He told me that my cat was not sick. Mittens was about to have kittens!

Now answer the questions about this part of the story.

(Comprehension continued)

DIRECTIONS: Listen to your teacher. Choose the correct answer.

3

(Comprehension continued)

DIRECTIONS: Listen to your teacher. Choose the correct answer.

4

○ ○ ○

5

○ ○ ○

(Comprehension continued)

DIRECTIONS: Read or listen to the story about Matt and his cat named Mittens.

Mittens (part 2)

9 When the five little kittens were born, I saw how small they were.

10 The kittens slept and drank all day in our apartment.

11 A basket kept the kittens safe and warm.

Mom told me I could pick one to keep. I tied a blue ribbon around my favorite kitten. I named my kitten Tiger.

The rest of Mittens' kittens now live with other girls and boys. I thank Mittens for letting me be part of her kitten family!

Now answer the questions about this part of the story.

(Comprehension continued)

DIRECTIONS: Listen to your teacher. Choose the correct answer.

6

○ ○ ○

7

○ ○ ○

8

○ ○ ○

(Comprehension continued)

DIRECTIONS: Listen to your teacher. Choose the correct answer.

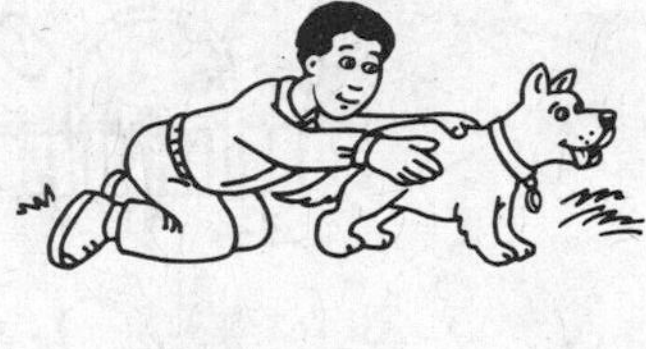

CHECKING SKILLS

DIRECTIONS: Listen to your teacher. Choose the correct answer.

11

12

13

(Checking Skills continued)

DIRECTIONS: Listen to your teacher. Choose the correct answer.

(Checking Skills continued)

DIRECTIONS: Listen to your teacher. Write the correct answer.

16 mittens looked sick.

17 cat small is the

18 The cat went to the vet.

(Checking Skills continued)

DIRECTIONS: Listen to your teacher. Write the correct answer.

19

The dog is ______________________________ .

20

Do you have a cat ________

WORD ANALYSIS

DIRECTIONS: Listen to your teacher. Choose the correct word.

21 dust ○ puck ○ duck ○

22 box ○ fox ○ foam ○

23 pets ○ pans ○ pies ○

(Word Analysis continued)

DIRECTIONS: Listen to your teacher. Choose the correct sentence.

24

- ○ I give the cat water.
- ○ The cat climbs trees.
- ○ I am the cat.

25

- ○ I help the dog.
- ○ I like fish.
- ○ I help and love the cat.

(Word Analysis continued)

DIRECTIONS: Listen to your teacher. Choose the word that makes the same vowel sound as the word you hear.

26

- ○ dad
- ○ lost
- ○ cake

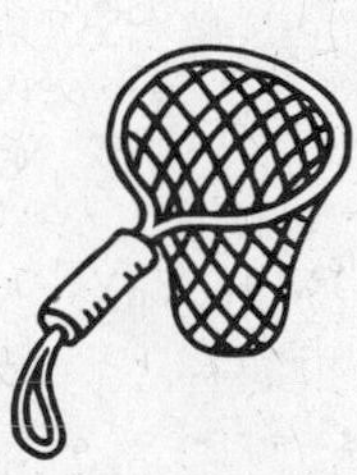

27

- ○ meet
- ○ no
- ○ vet

28

- ○ peg
- ○ big
- ○ pan

(Word Analysis continued)

DIRECTIONS: Listen to your teacher. Choose the word that makes the same vowel sound as the word you hear.

29

- ○ **dot**
- ○ **rip**
- ○ **cat**

30

- ○ **sat**
- ○ **see**
- ○ **fun**

VOCABULARY

DIRECTIONS: Listen to your teacher. Read the sentences. Choose the correct answer.

31 The cat **drank** from her bowl.

○ ○ ○

32 I take care of my **pet.**

○ ○ ○

33 The vet **examined** the dog.

○ ○ ○

(Vocabulary continued)

DIRECTIONS: Listen to your teacher. Read the sentences. Choose the correct answer.

34 We saw **boats** on the water.

○ ○ ○

35 The **hiker** walked far.

○ ○ ○

(Vocabulary continued)

DIRECTIONS: Listen to your teacher. Write the correct word.

36

37

38

39

40

WRITING

DIRECTIONS: Listen to your teacher. Draw on page 24. Write on page 25. Use the checklist on page 27 for help.

PROMPT

In "Mittens," Matt takes care of a cat that has kittens. Think of a pet you have or would like to have someday.

- What type of animal is your pet, or what type of animal would you like for a pet?
- How do you, or would you, take care of this pet?
- Tell about your pet and how you take care of it.

Draw a picture of you taking care of your pet. Then, write two complete sentences about it.

Matt takes good care of Mittens.

Draw your picture here.

Write your sentences here.

THIS PAGE LEFT INTENTIONALLY BLANK

(Writing continued)

WRITING CHECKLIST

Put a ✓ check next to the things you did.

Did you:

- ☐ draw you and your pet?
- ☐ think about your pet before writing?
- ☐ tell about how to take care of this pet?

Do your sentences:

- ☐ make sense?
- ☐ begin with a capital letter?
- ☐ end with a punctuation mark?

Remember to:

- ☐ look at your drawing.
- ☐ write two complete sentences.
- ☐ reread your sentences.

NAME ______________________________ DATE ______________

Progress Monitoring Assessment

Unit 2 Test

People in Communities

Glenview, Illinois • Boston, Massachusetts • Chandler, Arizona • Upper Saddle River, New Jersey

ISBN-13: 978-0-328-63453-8
ISBN-10: 0-328-63453-0

1 2 3 4 5 6 7 8 9 10 V0N4 14 13 12 11 10

COMPREHENSION

DIRECTIONS: Read or listen to the story about Kate and her bike.

A Bike for Kate

Kate saw a new bike at the bike shop. The bike was green. It had a bell. "I like that bike," said Kate.

"We cannot get that bike," said Mom.

But Mom found another bike.

Mom said, "This bike is old. But I can make it look new."

"I will wash the bike and paint it green."

The bike was very nice now because Mom fixed it up. The bike even had a new bell! Kate gave Mom a big hug.

Now answer the questions about this part of the story.

(Comprehension continued)

DIRECTIONS: Listen to your teacher. Choose the correct answer.

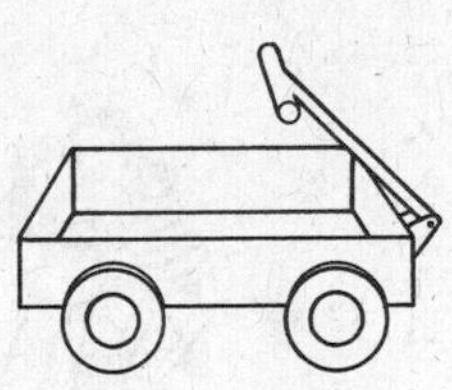

○ ○ ○

3

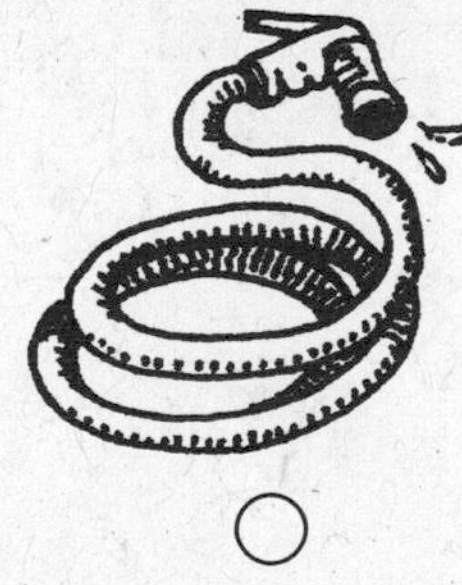

○ ○ ○

(Comprehension continued)

DIRECTIONS: Listen to your teacher. Choose the correct answer.

(Comprehension continued)

The Bike Path (part 2)

Kate and Mom rode their bikes to the bike path.

But the path had huge holes. Litter was on the ground.

"We need to fix the path," said Mom.

Mom and Kate asked people to help them.

People put cans for trash close to the path. People tossed grass seeds on the sides of the path. Soon grass was growing. Now the path is a good place to ride bikes.

Now answer the questions about this part of the story.

(Comprehension continued)

DIRECTIONS: Listen to your teacher. Choose the correct answer.

6

7

8

(Comprehension continued)

DIRECTIONS: Listen to your teacher. Choose the correct answer.

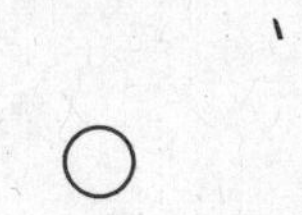

10

CHECKING SKILLS

DIRECTIONS: Listen to your teacher. Choose the correct word.

11 gave ○ big ○ hug ○

12 shop ○ bike ○ Kate ○

13 bikes ○ path ○ place ○

(Checking Skills continued)

DIRECTIONS: Listen to your teacher. Choose the correct answer.

14

- ◯ **one**
- ◯ **two**
- ◯ **three**

15

- ◯ **seeds**
- ◯ **sides**
- ◯ **path**

(Checking Skills continued)

DIRECTIONS: Listen to your teacher. Write the correct answer.

16 Litter was on the ground.

17 The bike was for Kate.

18 The bike was very nice now because Mom painted it.

(Checking Skills continued)

DIRECTIONS: Listen to your teacher. Circle the word or words that tell the correct answer.

19 Soon grass was growing.

20 kate, rick, and matt picked up litter.

WORD ANALYSIS

DIRECTIONS: Listen to your teacher. Choose the correct word.

21 **sip** ○ **ship** ○ **shop** ○

22 **cube** ○ **curl** ○ **cub** ○

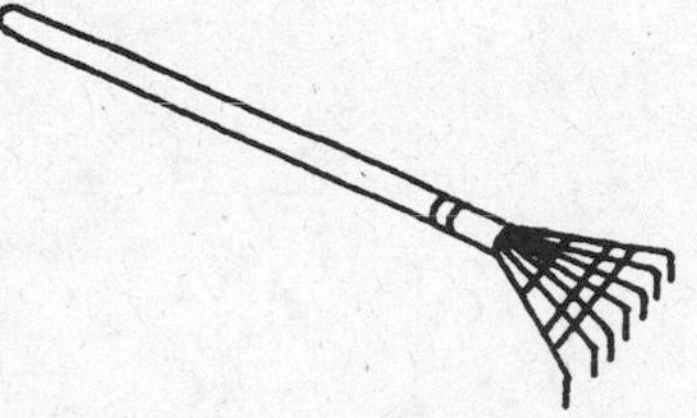

23 **rack** ○ **lake** ○ **rake** ○

(Word Analysis continued)

DIRECTIONS: Listen to your teacher. Choose the correct word.

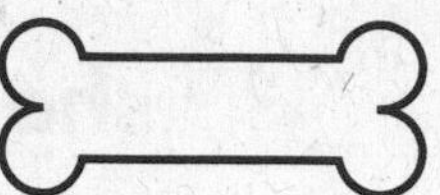

24
- ○ bun
- ○ bone
- ○ dome

25
- ○ sheet
- ○ shape
- ○ sheep

(Word Analysis continued)

DIRECTIONS: Listen to your teacher. Circle the correct words.

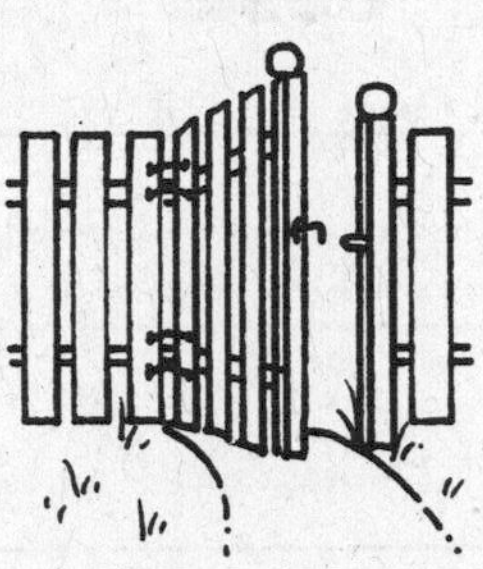

26 Jan will take me to the game.

27 Do you like to hike and swim?

28 Jason sent a note to his brother at home.

(Word Analysis continued)

DIRECTIONS: Listen to your teacher. Write the letters that make the beginning sound. Then write the word.

29

____ ____ **eese**

____

30

____ ____ **ale**

____

VOCABULARY

DIRECTIONS: Listen to your teacher. Read the sentences. Choose the correct answer.

31 These **insects** have wings and six legs.

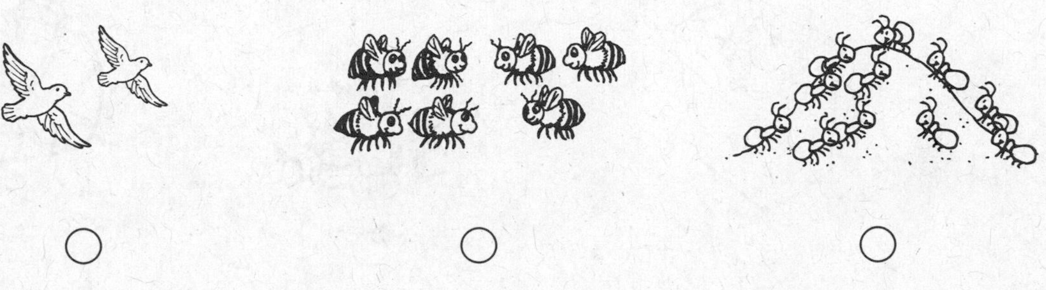

32 The box is **under** the bed.

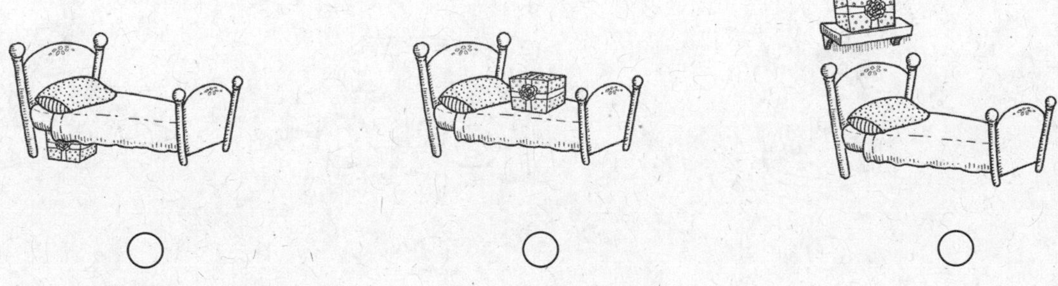

33 The **family** sat down to eat a **meal.**

(Vocabulary continued)

DIRECTIONS: Listen to your teacher. Read the sentences. Choose the correct answer.

34 **Litter** is on the **ground.**

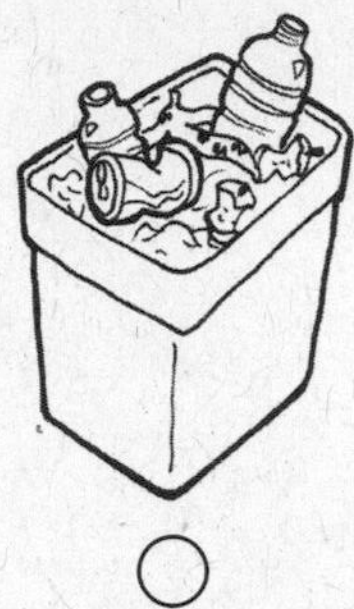

○

○

○

---

35 Ben can **wash** the dish.

○

○

○

(Vocabulary continued)

DIRECTIONS: Listen to your teacher. Write the correct answer.

bees	gather	hole	nurse	return

36 Flying insects that make honey and can sting you are

______________________________.

37 An empty space or opening in something is a

______________________________.

38 Someone who is trained to help doctors and take care of people who are sick and injured is a

______________________________.

39 To come together in a group is to

______________________________.

40 To come back or to go back to a place is to

______________________________.

WRITING

DIRECTIONS: Listen to your teacher. Draw on page 24. Write on page 25. Use the checklist on page 27 for help.

PROMPT

Mom helps Kate in "A Bike for Kate" by fixing up a bike for Kate.

Think about your family.

- **How do people in your family help you?**
- **How do you help people in your family?**

Draw a picture that shows these things. Then, write at least two complete sentences about it.

Here is Kate's mom making the old bike look new.

Draw your picture here.

Write your sentences here.

THIS PAGE LEFT INTENTIONALLY BLANK

(Writing continued)

WRITING CHECKLIST

Put a ✓ check next to the things you did.

Did you:

- ☐ draw your family members helping?
- ☐ think about how family members help each other before writing?
- ☐ tell what you or family members do to help?

Do your sentences:

- ☐ make sense?
- ☐ begin with a capital letter?
- ☐ end with a punctuation mark?

Remember to:

- ☐ look at your drawing.
- ☐ write at least two complete sentences.
- ☐ reread your sentences.

NAME ______________________ DATE ______________

Progress Monitoring Assessment

Unit 3 Test

Growing and Changing

Glenview, Illinois • Boston, Massachusetts • Chandler, Arizona • Upper Saddle River, New Jersey

ISBN-13: 978-0-328-63454-5
ISBN-10: 0-328-63454-9

1 2 3 4 5 6 7 8 9 10 V0N4 14 13 12 11 10

COMPREHENSION

DIRECTIONS: Read or listen to the story about Lin and her friends.

Rainy Day Picnic

1 Lin and two friends were playing in the park.

2 The girls had food in their bags.

3 The girls planned to eat outside.

4 "The sky is cloudy," Lin said. "Do you think it will rain?"

5 Soon the girls could feel big drops of water.

6 It was raining!

7 The girls picked up their bags.
They ran with Lin's mom into the building.

8 "What can we do?" said Lin.

"We can't eat outside," said Lin's mom. "But we can eat inside."

First, the girls put a cloth down. Then they sat down. Next, the girls ate their food. The girls had fun eating inside.

Now answer the questions about the story.

(Comprehension continued)

DIRECTIONS: Listen to your teacher. Choose the correct answer.

1

○ ○ ○

2

○ ○ ○

(Comprehension continued)

DIRECTIONS: Listen to your teacher. Choose the correct sentence.

○ The sky was cloudy.
○ The girls got wet.
○ The girls could not eat outside.

○ The girls ate inside.
○ The girls rode their bikes home.
○ The girls waited for the sun to shine.

○ The girls sat down.
○ The girls ate their food.
○ The girls put a cloth down.

(Comprehension continued)

DIRECTIONS: Read or listen to the story about how to make ice pops.

Making Ice Pops

You can make ice pops. Here is what you do. First, get five small paper cups. Then put fruit juice in the cups. Put the cups inside the freezer. Wait one hour. Then put sticks inside the cups.

7 Freeze the cups for one day.

8 Take a cup out of the freezer.

9 Then peel the paper cup off the ice pop.

10 Last, eat your ice pop.

Now answer the questions about the story.

(Comprehension continued)

DIRECTIONS: Listen to your teacher. Choose the correct answer.

6

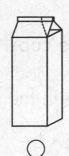

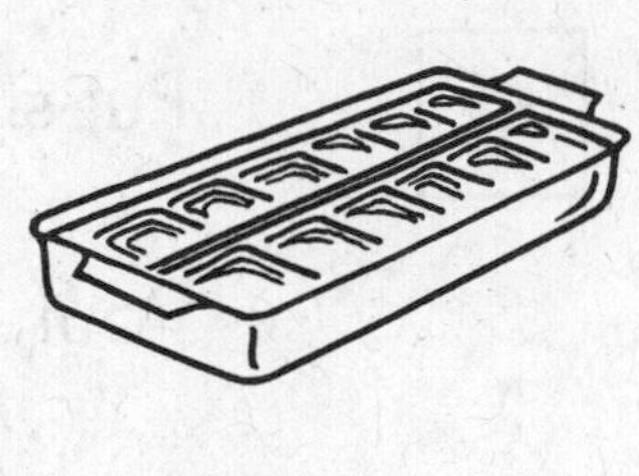

○ ○ ○

7

○  

8

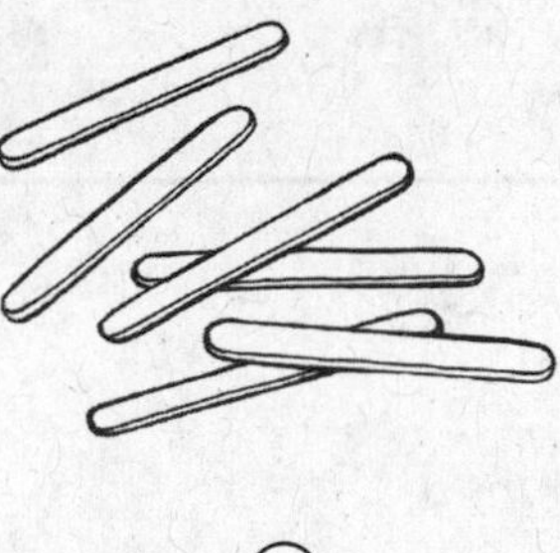

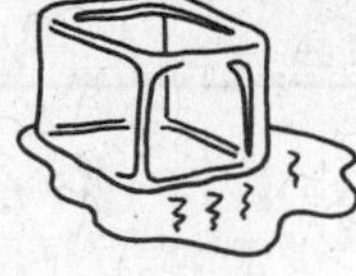

○ ○ 

(Comprehension continued)

DIRECTIONS: Listen to your teacher. Choose the correct answer.

9

○ Put sticks in the cups.

○ Pour fruit juice in the cups.

○ Take a drink.

10

○ Peel off the paper cups.

○ Eat the ice pops.

○ Fill the cups.

CHECKING SKILLS

DIRECTIONS: Listen to your teacher. Choose the correct answer.

11 First, the girls put a cloth down.

- ○ **First**
- ○ **put**
- ○ **down**

---

12 Then they sat down.

- ○ **they**
- ○ **sat**
- ○ **down**

---

13 Next, the girls ate their food.

- ○ **girls**
- ○ **ate**
- ○ **food**

(Checking Skills continued)

DIRECTIONS: Listen to your teacher. Choose the correct answer.

14 "We can't eat outside," said Lin's mom.

- ○ **can't**
- ○ **outside**
- ○ **said**

15 The girls picked up their bags.

- ○ **girls**
- ○ **picked**
- ○ **their**

(Checking Skills continued)

DIRECTIONS: Listen to your teacher. Write the correct word.

16

packs packed

The girls ______________ their bags.

17

walk walked

Lin ______________ into the building.

18

played playing

The girls ______________ tag.

(Checking Skills continued)

DIRECTIONS: Listen to your teacher. Write the correct word.

first	now	pets

19

Dogs are ______________ .

Cats are ______________ .

20

At ______________ , I was small.

______________ , I am big.

WORD ANALYSIS

DIRECTIONS: Listen to your teacher. Choose the correct word.

21 ship ○ sink ○ shark ○

22 firefighter ○ fire truck ○ campfire ○

23 store ○ stare ○ sort ○

(Word Analysis continued)

DIRECTIONS: Listen to your teacher. Choose the correct word.

24

- ○ **wheel**
- ○ **wagon**
- ○ **wagging**

25

- ○ **bed**
- ○ **bird**
- ○ **burn**

(Word Analysis continued)

DIRECTIONS: Listen to your teacher. Circle the plural words that end in *-es*.

26 Cups and glasses are dishes.

27 Foxes live in dens.

28 Do we need passes to get on the buses?

(Word Analysis continued)

DIRECTIONS: Listen to your teacher. Write the correct word.

29 **hop** **hopped** **hopping**

I was ______________ like a little bird.

30 **turn** **turned** **turning**

Dad ______________ the pages as he read to me.

VOCABULARY

DIRECTIONS: Listen to your teacher. Read the sentences. Choose the correct answer.

31 The girl **stands.**

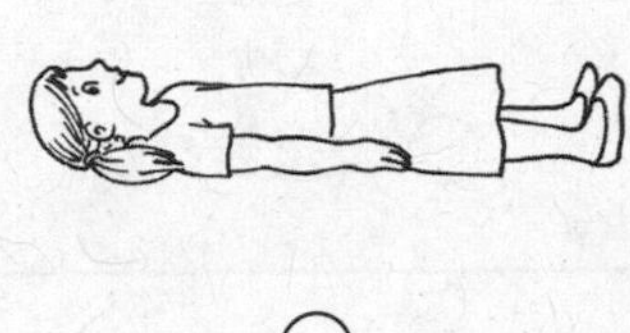

○ ○ ○

32 The sky is **cloudy** today.

○ ○ ○

(Vocabulary continued)

DIRECTIONS: Listen to your teacher. Choose the correct answer.

33

○ **school** ○ **house** ○ **building**

34

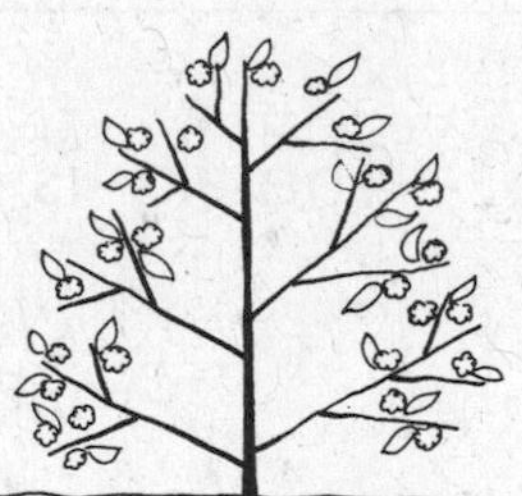

○ **geese** ○ **birds** ○ **spring**

35

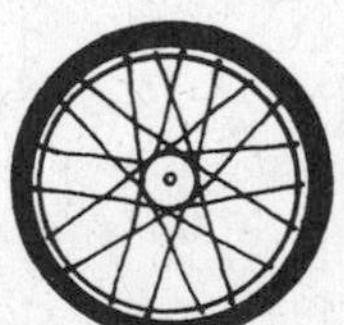

○ **car** ○ **bicycle** ○ **wheels**

(Vocabulary continued)

DIRECTIONS: Listen to your teacher. Write the correct word.

36

37

38

39

40

WRITING

DIRECTIONS: Listen to your teacher. Draw on page 24. Write on page 25. Use the checklist on page 27 for help.

PROMPT

In "Rainy Day Picnic," Lin and her friends wanted to eat outside. It rained, so the girls changed their plans.

- **Tell about a time you changed your plans.**
- **What did you want to do?**
- **Why did you change plans?**
- **Then tell what you did do.**

Draw a picture showing a time you changed plans. Then write at least two sentences about it.

Here is what happened when Lin and her friends had to change plans.

Draw your picture here.

Write your sentences here.

THIS PAGE LEFT INTENTIONALLY BLANK

(Writing continued)

WRITING CHECKLIST

Put a ✓ check next to the things you did.

Did you:

- ☐ draw a picture showing a time you changed plans?
- ☐ think about a time when you had to change your plans?
- ☐ tell what you wanted to do, and what you did do?

Do your sentences:

- ☐ make sense?
- ☐ begin with a capital letter?
- ☐ end with a punctuation mark?

Remember to:

- ☐ look at your drawing.
- ☐ write at least two complete sentences.
- ☐ reread your sentences.

NAME ________________________________ DATE ______________

Progress Monitoring Assessment

Unit 4 Test

Surprising Treasures

Glenview, Illinois • Boston, Massachusetts • Chandler, Arizona • Upper Saddle River, New Jersey

ISBN-13: 978-0-328-63455-2
ISBN-10: 0-328-63455-7

1 2 3 4 5 6 7 8 9 10 V0N4 14 13 12 11 10

COMPREHENSION

DIRECTIONS: Read or listen to the story about Felix.

Happy Birthday, America!

Felix looked at the calendar. There was a big, red circle around July 4. Felix and his family were having a birthday party for the United States.

4 Felix sent cards to the neighbors.

5 Ana hung red, white, and blue banners on the gate.

6 Dad set up a big table in the yard.

Mom made tacos. Ana put tomatoes on a plate. Jack roasted corn on the grill. Mr. Lee made a rice dish. Mrs. Lee brought fruit.

Now answer the questions about this part of the story.

(Comprehension continued)

DIRECTIONS: Listen to your teacher. Choose the correct answer.

1

2

3

(Comprehension continued)

(Comprehension continued)

Happy Birthday, America! (part 2)

Grandpa told stories about when he was a little boy. Grandpa lived on a small farm in Mexico. Mr. Lee showed pictures of the city in China where he grew up.

The neighbors went to the Fourth of July parade. They saw marching bands. They waved flags.

Soon it was dark. But the party was not over. Bright fireworks filled the sky. Felix was glad to celebrate this special day.

Now answer the questions about this part of the story.

(Comprehension continued)

DIRECTIONS: Listen to your teacher. Choose the correct answer.

6

7

8

(Comprehension continued)

DIRECTIONS: Listen to your teacher. Choose the correct answer.

9

apartment ○ **house in the woods** ○ **farm** ○

10

mad ○ **happy** ○ **sad** ○

CHECKING SKILLS

DIRECTIONS: Listen to your teacher. Choose the correct answer.

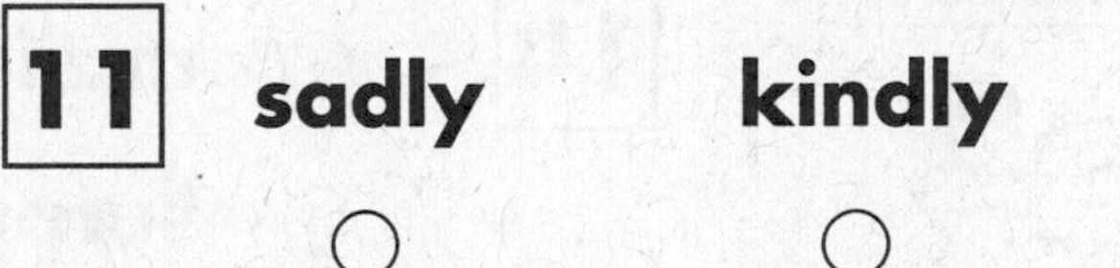

11 sadly ○ kindly ○ slowly ○

12 baked ○ skipped ○ jumped ○

13 loudly ○ softly ○ shortly ○

(Checking Skills continued)

DIRECTIONS: Listen to your teacher. Choose the correct answer.

- ○ **mailed**
- ○ **surprised**
- ○ **tossed**

- ○ **jumped**
- ○ **snapped**
- ○ **laughed**

(Checking Skills continued)

DIRECTIONS: Listen to your teacher. Write a sentence that describes the picture.

16

17

18

(Checking Skills continued)

DIRECTIONS: Look at the pictures. Listen to your teacher. Write a word to finish each sentence.

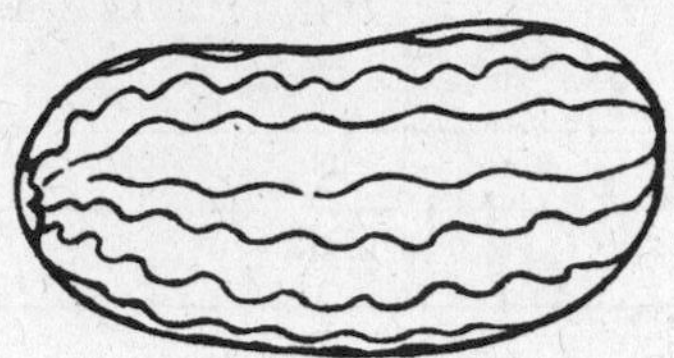

19 The watermelon is ____________ than the apple.

20 The mouse is ____________ than the elephant.

WORD ANALYSIS

DIRECTIONS: Listen to your teacher. Choose the correct word.

21 soil ○ side ○ sail ○

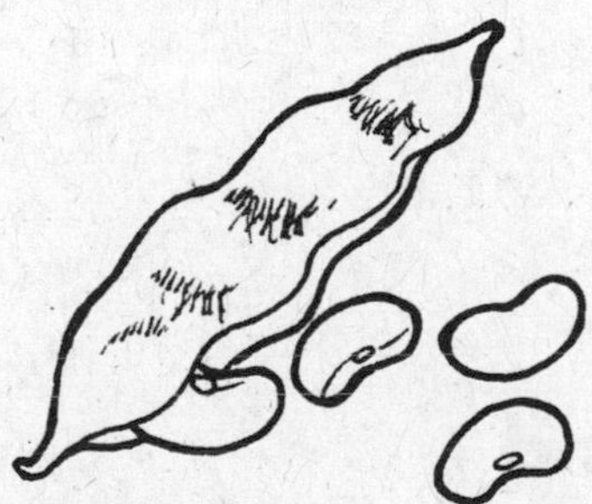

22 bean ○ band ○ bend ○

23 cane ○ coat ○ cot ○

(Word Analysis continued)

DIRECTIONS: Listen to your teacher. Choose the correct word.

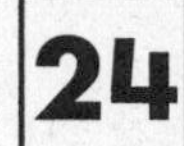

24

- ○ footstep
- ○ rainbow
- ○ snowman

25

- ○ doorbell
- ○ airplane
- ○ playground

(Word Analysis continued)

DIRECTIONS: Listen to your teacher. Write the correct word.

26

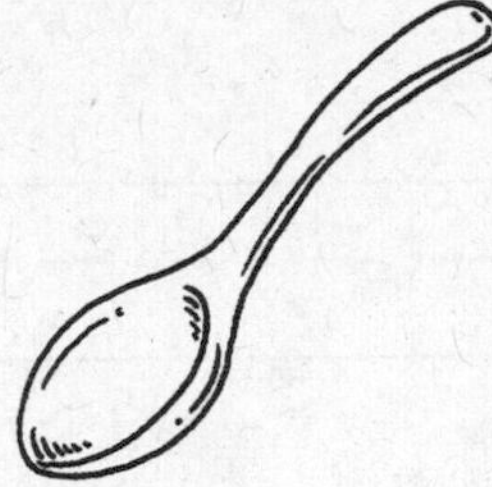

27

28

(Word Analysis continued)

DIRECTIONS: Listen to your teacher. Write the correct word.

29

30

VOCABULARY

DIRECTIONS: Listen to your teacher. Choose the correct answer.

31 Ann saw the **moon** shining in the evening sky.

○ ○ ○

32 I grew vegetables in my **garden.**

○ ○ ○

33 We gave Tom a **surprise** party for his birthday.

○ ○ ○

(Vocabulary continued)

DIRECTIONS: Listen to your teacher. Choose the correct answer.

34 There was an American **flag** in front of the post office.

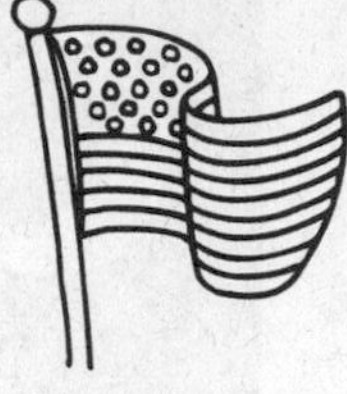

35 José made a **card** for his mother.

(Vocabulary continued)

DIRECTIONS: Listen to your teacher. Write the correct word.

36

37

38

39

40

WRITING

DIRECTIONS: Listen to your teacher. Draw on page 24. Write on page 25. Use the checklist on page 27 for help.

PROMPT

In "Happy Birthday, America!" Felix, his family, and his neighbors celebrated our country's birthday.

Think of a special celebration you have shared.

- What did you do?
- How did you help?

Draw a picture of what happened. Then tell what happened in two complete sentences.

Here is Felix celebrating the Fourth of July with his family and neighbors.

Draw your picture here.

Write your sentences here.

THIS PAGE LEFT INTENTIONALLY BLANK

(Writing continued)

WRITING CHECKLIST

Put a ✓ check next to the things you did.

Did you:

- ☐ draw the celebration you had?
- ☐ think about a special celebration you have shared?
- ☐ tell what you did and how you helped?

Do your sentences:

- ☐ make sense?
- ☐ begin with a capital letter?
- ☐ end with a punctuation mark?

Remember to:

- ☐ look at your drawing.
- ☐ write at least two complete sentences.
- ☐ reread your sentences.

NAME ______________________________ DATE ______________

Progress Monitoring Assessment

Unit 5 Test

Clever Solutions

Glenview, Illinois • Boston, Massachusetts • Chandler, Arizona • Upper Saddle River, New Jersey

ISBN-13: 978-0-328-63456-9
ISBN-10: 0-328-63456-5

1 2 3 4 5 6 7 8 9 10 V0N4 14 13 12 11 10

COMPREHENSION

DIRECTIONS: Read or listen to the story about an invention that changed the world.

An Invention That Changed the World

1 Can you imagine a time before computers, television, or telephones?

2 What would your life be like without these amazing inventions?

3 Computers help us talk to people all over the world.

4 Television helps us learn things and have fun.

5 Airplanes changed the way we travel forever.

Before airplanes, people could not travel long distances easily. They used wagons on land and boats on the sea. It could take many days or weeks to go from one place to another.

Orville Wright and his brother Wilbur made the first airplane. Their first flight was over 100 years ago. The flight lasted only a few seconds. But their invention would soon change the world!

Now answer the questions about this part of the story.

(Comprehension continued)

DIRECTIONS: Listen to your teacher. Choose the correct answer.

1

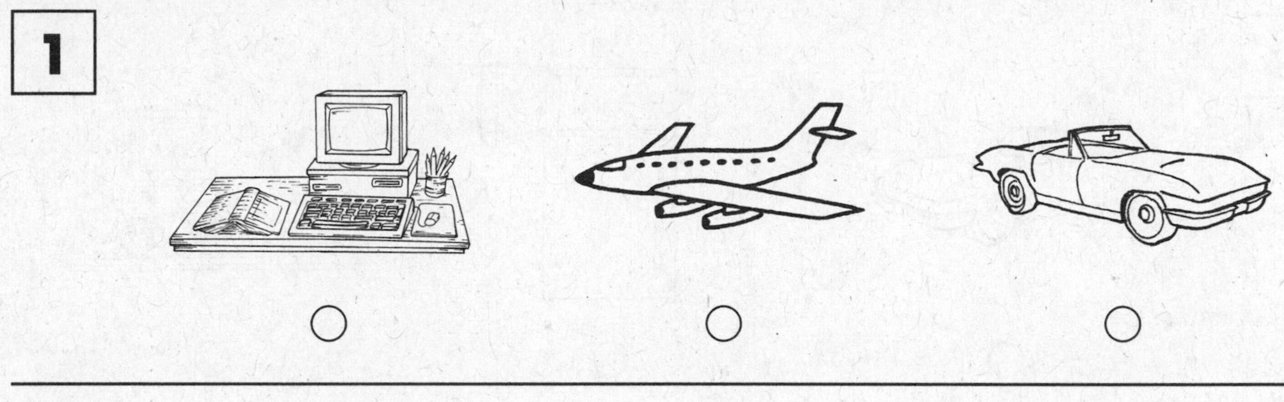

2

3

(Comprehension continued)

DIRECTIONS: Listen to your teacher. Choose the correct answer.

4

5

(Comprehension continued)

DIRECTIONS: Read or listen to the story about an invention that changed the world.

An Invention That Changed the World (part 2)

Orville and Wilbur Wright sold bicycles before they were inventors. They read books and watched birds fly. They worked hard for many years. The first airplane was named *Flyer.*

The Wright Brothers' invention changed how people travel. Long ago, it could take many days or weeks to cross the ocean. Today, an airplane ride across the ocean takes only hours. Maybe someday you will invent something that will change lives, just like the Wright Brothers!

Now answer the questions about this part of the story.

(Comprehension continued)

DIRECTIONS: Listen to your teacher. Choose the correct answer.

(Comprehension continued)

DIRECTIONS: Listen to your teacher. Choose the correct answer.

9

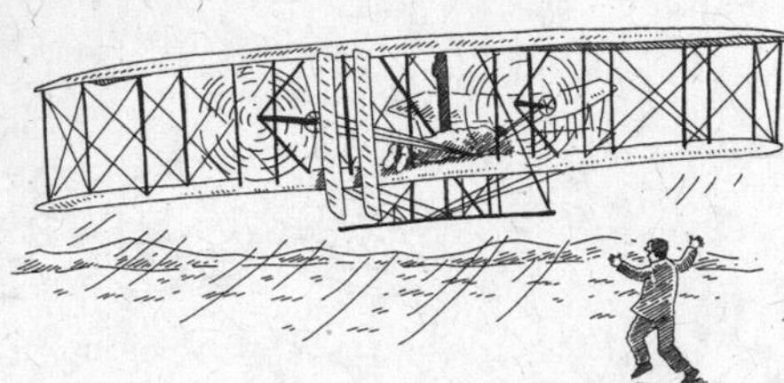

○ It was a bicycle.

○ It was an airplane.

○ It was a boat.

10

○ a car

○ a ship

○ an airplane

CHECKING SKILLS

DIRECTIONS: Listen to your teacher. Choose the correct answer.

11

12

13

(Checking Skills continued)

DIRECTIONS: Listen to your teacher. Choose the correct answer.

14

15

○ ○ ○

(Checking Skills continued)

DIRECTIONS: Listen to your teacher. Write the correct punctuation mark.

16

Do you see the airplane ______

17

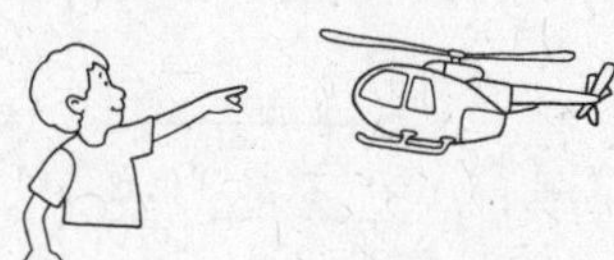

Look at that ______

18

May I sit by the window ______

(Checking Skills continued)

DIRECTIONS: Listen to your teacher. Write the correct punctuation mark.

Pack your suitcase ______

The airplane is loud ______

WORD ANALYSIS

DIRECTIONS: Listen to your teacher. Choose the correct word.

21 crow ○ cow ○ car ○

22 mouse ○ mask ○ mow ○

23 hike ○ hook ○ hat ○

(Word Analysis continued)

DIRECTIONS: Listen to your teacher. Choose the correct word.

24

- ○ renew
- ○ repack
- ○ reread

25

- ○ unwrap
- ○ unhappy
- ○ unstuck

(Word Analysis continued)

DIRECTIONS: Listen to your teacher. Write the correct word.

26

27

28

(Word Analysis continued)

DIRECTIONS: Listen to your teacher. Write the correct word.

29

30

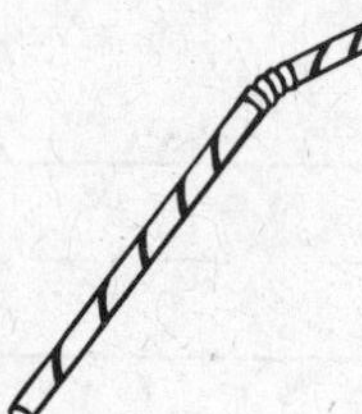

VOCABULARY

DIRECTIONS: Listen to your teacher. Read the sentences. Choose the correct answer.

31 The bee **flew** to the flower.

○ ○ ○

32 Pam was **upside down** on the beam.

○ ○ ○

33 The boy **pulled** the fish out of the water.

○ ○ ○

(Vocabulary continued)

DIRECTIONS: Listen to your teacher. Read the sentences. Choose the correct answer.

34 The **closet** was full of clothes.

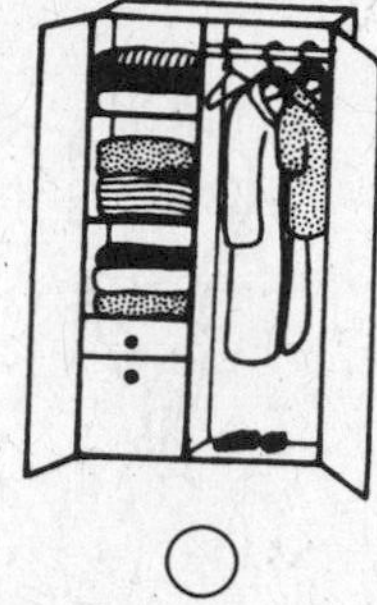

○ ○ ○

35 Bill bent down to **retie** his shoe.

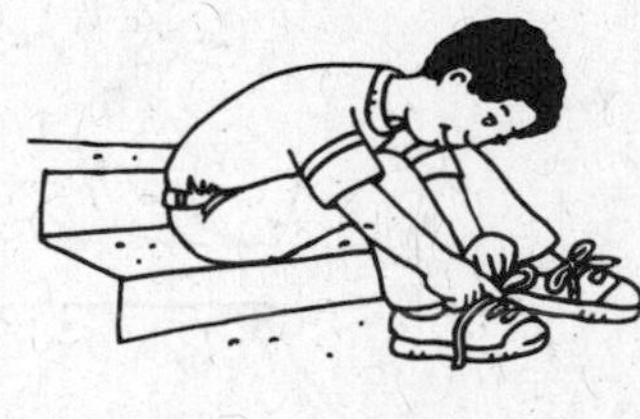

○ ○ ○

(Vocabulary continued)

DIRECTIONS: Listen to your teacher. Write the correct word.

36

37

38

39

40

WRITING

DIRECTIONS: Listen to your teacher. Draw on page 24. Write on page 25. Use the checklist on page 27 for help.

PROMPT

In "An Invention That Changed the World," the Wright Brothers invented the airplane to make travel easier.

Think of an invention you use that makes your life easier.

- **What is the invention?**
- **How do you use it?**
- **How does the invention make your life easier?**

Draw the invention. Then write three complete sentences.

The Wright Brothers' invention, the airplane, changed the world.

Draw your picture here.

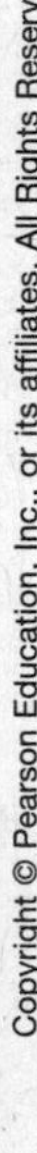

Write your sentences here.

THIS PAGE LEFT INTENTIONALLY BLANK

(Writing continued)

WRITING CHECKLIST

Put a ✓ check next to the things you did.

Did you:

- ☐ draw an invention?
- ☐ think about an invention that makes your life easier?
- ☐ tell how you use the invention?

Do your sentences:

- ☐ make sense?
- ☐ begin with a capital letter?
- ☐ end with a punctuation mark?

Remember to:

- ☐ look at your drawing.
- ☐ write three complete sentences.
- ☐ reread your sentences.